Miraculous Magic Tricks

PAPER MAGIC

by Mike Lane

Illustrations by David Mostyn

WINDMILL BOOKS™

New York

Published in 2012 by Windmill Books, an Imprint of Rosen Publishing
29 East 21st Street, New York, NY 10010

Copyright © 2012 by Arcturus Publishing Ltd.

First Edition

Author: Mike Lane
Editors: Patience Coster and Joe Harris
Illustrations: David Mostyn
Design: Tokiko Morishima

Library of Congress Cataloging-in-Publication Data

Lane, Mike.
 Paper magic / by Mike Lane.
   p. cm. — (Miraculous magic tricks)
 Includes index.
 ISBN 978-1-61533-511-4 (library binding) — ISBN 978-1-
4488-6729-5 (pbk.) — ISBN 978-1-4488-6730-1 (6-pack)
 1. Magic tricks. 2. Paper. I. Title.
 GV1547.L285 2012
 793.8—dc23
                              2011021766
Printed in China

CPSIA Compliance Information: Batch # AW2102WM: For further information
contact Windmill Books, New York, New York at 1-866-478-0556

SL002050US

CONTENTS

Introduction	4
The Magician's Pledge	5
Stepping through Paper	6
Magical Mend	9
Floating Cup	12
Paper Jump	14
A Tree from Paper	16
Overhead	18
Money Morph	21
Tic Tac Toe	24
Rip It, Restore It	26
Psychic Paper	29
Further Reading, Web Sites, Glossary, and Index	32

INTRODUCTION

Within these pages you will discover great paper tricks that are easy to do and impressive to watch.

To be a successful magician, you will need to practice the tricks in private before you perform them in front of an audience. An excellent way to practice is in front of a mirror, since you can watch the magic happen before your own eyes.

When performing, you must speak clearly, slowly, and loudly enough for everyone to hear. But never tell the audience what's going to happen.

Remember to "watch your angles." This means being careful about where your spectators are standing or sitting when you are performing. The best place is directly in front of you.

Never tell the secret of how the trick is done. If someone asks, just say: "It's magic!"

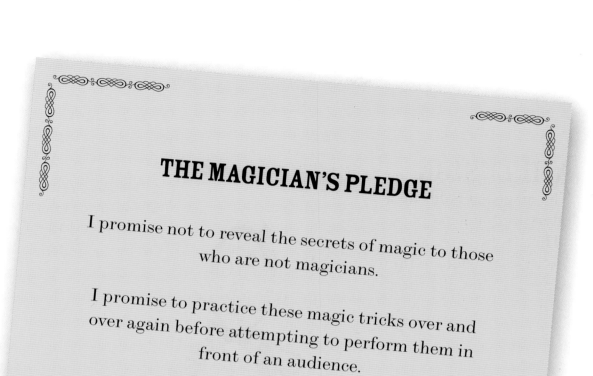

THE MAGICIAN'S PLEDGE

I promise not to reveal the secrets of magic to those who are not magicians.

I promise to practice these magic tricks over and over again before attempting to perform them in front of an audience.

I promise to respect my art, the art of magic.

STEPPING THROUGH PAPER

ILLUSION

The magician holds up a letter-sized sheet of paper. He tells the spectator he will cut a hole in the paper big enough to step through, and he does.

1 The magician folds the paper in half lengthwise.

2 Starting approximately ½ inch (1 cm) down from the top edge, the magician cuts in a straight line from the crease to the open edge, stopping just before the edge. He must be careful NOT to cut right across!

3 Now he makes a second cut from the open edge toward the crease, starting ½ inch (1 cm) below the first cut and stopping just before the crease in the same way.

4 He continues this back and forth, cutting until he reaches ½ inch (1 cm) from the bottom edge of the paper.

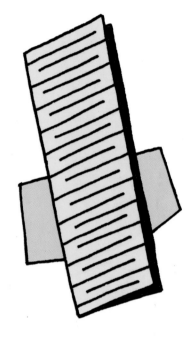

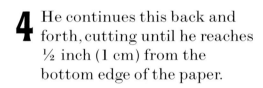

5 Once he has finished cutting, he opens the page carefully. He now cuts all the folds down the spine of the page APART from those at the top and the bottom.

MAGIC TIP!
REMEMBER TO CHANGE DIRECTION WITH EACH CUT ACROSS THE PAGE OR YOUR CIRCLE WON'T WORK! PRACTICE THIS TRICK AND YOU'LL SOON BE A CUT ABOVE THE REST OF THE MAGICIANS.

6 The paper should now form a large circle. The magician carefully steps through the hole in the paper.

MAGICAL MEND

ILLUSION

The magician cuts a column of print from a newspaper, folds it, cuts it, and then restores it to its uncut form.

1 Prior to the trick, the magician prepares the newspaper by cutting out a long column of print.

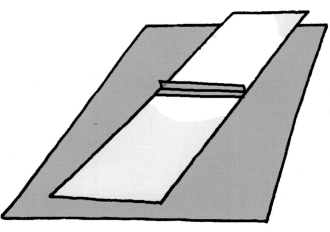

2 He sticks the two ends of a piece of adhesive tape together to make a loop, then sticks it in the middle of the back of the column. The spectator will not see this reverse side of the paper.

3 To perform the trick, the magician holds the newspaper column up so that the spectator sees the front of it.

4 The magician folds the newspaper column in half from top to bottom. He folds it toward himself so that the tape holds the two surfaces together.

5 With a pair of scissors, he cuts the folded newspaper just under the fold but not ON it.

6 The magician holds the bottom edge of the paper, and folds the other half up toward the audience. Because the tape is holding the two sides together, it will appear that the paper is still in one piece.

FLOATING CUP

ILLUSION
The magician holds
a cup in his hands.
He lets go of it
slowly and it remains
floating in mid-air.

1 Prior to the trick, the
magician takes a large paper
or foam cup and pokes a hole
halfway up with his thumb.

2 To perform the trick,
he picks up the cup
with both hands, with
the hole facing him.

3 He wraps his fingers
round the sides of the cup
and inserts a thumb into
the hole from behind.

4 The magician now loosens his grip and slowly wiggles his fingers close to the cup. From the spectator's side it will look as though the cup is floating. The magician must be sure the spectator cannot see the cup from behind.

5 The magician once again grips the cup with his fingers, removes his thumb from the hole, and puts the cup aside.

PAPER JUMP

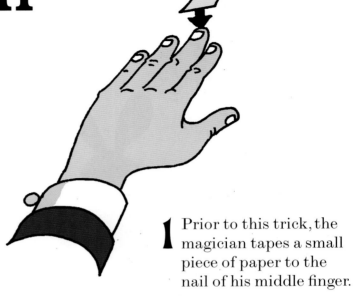

ILLUSION
A small piece of paper taped to the magician's fingernail jumps back and forth between two fingers.

1 Prior to this trick, the magician tapes a small piece of paper to the nail of his middle finger.

2 The magician places his middle and index fingers of this hand on the edge of a table with the thumb and remaining fingers curled under.

3 The magician lifts the fingers to his shoulder, curls in his index finger, and sticks out his ring finger. This movement is done quickly.

4 The magician brings his fingers back down to the edge of the table. The spectators will be amazed as it will look as though the paper has jumped from one finger to the other.

MAGIC TIP!
THIS TRICK CAN BE REPEATED OVER AND OVER, MAKING IT LOOK AS THOUGH THE PAPER IS JUMPING BACK AND FORTH. THE QUICKER IT IS DONE, THE BETTER IT LOOKS.

5 The magician lifts his hand to his shoulder again. Switching his fingers back to the starting position, he brings them back down onto the table.

A TREE FROM PAPER

1 The magician takes a sheet of newspaper and rolls it into a tube.

2 With a pair of scissors, he cuts a slit from the top of one side to about halfway down.

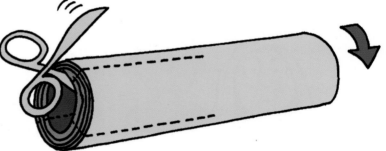

3 He does this twice more, keeping the space between the slits equal.

4 He allows the
sides to fall down.

5 Then he pulls out
the paper from the
middle of the tube.

6 A tree has grown,
from paper.

OVERHEAD

1 The magician asks a spectator to sit on a chair facing the audience.

2 The magician rolls up a paper tissue into a ball and shows it to the spectator and the audience.

3 The magician throws the tissue ball from hand to hand in front of the spectator.

4 The magician now quickly tosses the tissue ball over the spectator's head, but continues to act as though the ball is still going back and forth between both hands. Of course, the audience will see the tissue go over the spectator's head.

5 The magician now opens his hands and shows the puzzled spectator that the tissue ball has vanished.

MONEY MORPH

ILLUSION
A bill of one value is folded and changes (morphs) into a bill of different value when it is unfolded.

1 Prior to the trick, the magician takes two bills of different value and places one of them on a table.

2 He folds this bill in half from left to right.

3 Then he folds it in half again from left to right.

4 Now he folds it in half a third time, from top to bottom, to form a square.

5 He places the second bill on the table.

6 With a piece of sticky tape, he attaches the folded bill to the bottom right-hand corner of the second bill, with the creased side uppermost. The folded bill should be completely hidden behind the second bill.

7 The magician is now ready to perform. He holds up the bill for the spectators to see. The magician's right thumb covers the folded bill at the back and his fingers are held in front of the second bill. He holds the left-hand side of the bill with his left hand.

8 The magician folds the bill in half from left to right.

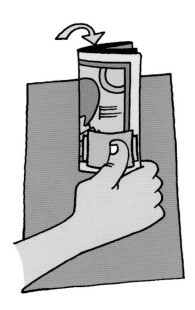

9 He folds it in half again the same way.

10 Then he folds it in half a third time, from top to bottom, being careful not to expose the hidden bill.

11 The magician quickly flips the bills over so that the back bill becomes the front bill and the front bill becomes the back bill.

12 Using both hands, he carefully unfolds the front bill (which was the back bill), being careful not to expose the back bill (which was the front bill). His hands should be in the same position as when the trick began.

TIC TAC TOE

ILLUSION

Three pieces of paper, two marked with an X and one marked with an O, are dropped into a bag. With his eyes closed, the magician can pick out any piece the spectator calls out.

1 On a sheet of paper, the magician draws a large X followed by a large O and then a large X. Each letter should take up one third of the page.

2 The magician folds the paper into three.

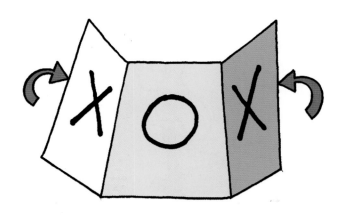

3 Now he tears the paper along the fold lines (the paper must not be cut with scissors).

4 The magician places the three pieces of paper in a bag and asks a spectator to call out "O" or "X."

5 The magician reaches into the bag and removes whichever letter is called out. He does this by feeling the edges of the long sides of the paper: the X pieces have one smooth, straight side and one torn side; the O piece has two torn sides.

RIP IT, RESTORE IT

ILLUSION

The magician shows the audience a page from a newspaper or magazine and proceeds to rip it into several pieces. He squeezes the pieces into a ball, unfolds the ball, and the paper is back in one piece.

1 Prior to the trick, the magician takes two duplicate pages from a newspaper or magazine. He crumples one page into a ball.

2 The magician hides the crumpled page behind the other page, holding it with his thumb against the top left-hand corner. He holds his fingers in front of the page, visible to the spectators.

3 With his right hand, the magician starts ripping the page into strips. Each time a strip is ripped, he places it in front of the area where the crumpled ball is hidden.

4 Once several strips have been ripped, the magician squeezes them together using both hands. He must be careful not to combine the ripped pieces with the pre-crumpled ball. At this point, there should be two paper balls in the magician's hands.

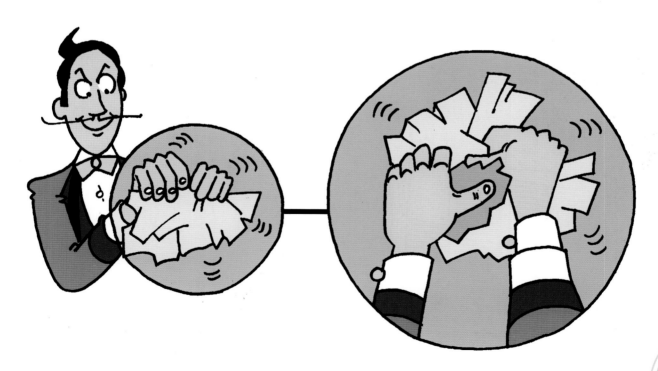

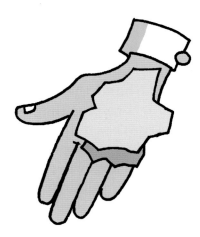

6 The ball of un-ripped paper should be on top.

5 The magician takes the paper balls in his right hand.

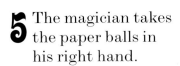

7 Slowly, the magician opens his hand and, keeping the ripped ball hidden, begins to unfold the un-ripped ball. He hides the ripped ball behind the open page, which appears to have been magically restored.

PSYCHIC PAPER

ILLUSION

The magician attempts to read the spectator's minds while they are thinking of an item. The magician writes down the item he believes they are thinking of. At first, the spectators think the magician has failed, but he proves at the end of the trick that he got them all correct.

1 The magician needs four spectators to assist with this trick. One of them is secretly part of the trick. Before the trick, the magician tells his secret assistant to say "apples" in answer to his question.

APPLES

2 The magician has a pen, a pad, and a clear plastic bag. He asks a spectator (not his secret assistant, who will be fourth) to silently think of an item from a grocery store. He acts as if he is reading the spectator's mind and writes down the word "apples."

3 The magician asks the spectator what item they were thinking of. Let's imagine that they say "milk." The magician looks disappointed, rips the page from the pad, and crumples it into a ball. He puts the ball in the plastic bag. He does not show the spectators what he wrote before crumpling the page into a ball.

4 The magician now turns to the second spectator. He tells them to: "Think of an item and look into my eyes." He writes down the item the first spectator said (in our example, "milk"). The magician asks the second spectator what their item was (let's say it was "bread"). Again the magician looks disappointed, rips out the page from the pad, crumples it into a ball, and throws it in the plastic bag.

MILK

5 The magicians now asks the third spectator the same question. He writes down the item the second spectator said (in our example, "bread"). Once again the magician asks what the item was (let's say it was "toothpaste"). He again looks disappointed, rips, crumples, and tosses the page into the bag.

BREAD

6 Finally, the magician asks his secret assistant to think of an item. He writes down the item the third spectator said (in our example, "toothpaste"). He asks the secret assistant what the item was. Of course the item will be apples. Once again the magician, rips, crumples, and tosses the page into the bag.

TOOTHPASTE

7 The magician now announces, "I never said I got the answers wrong!" He removes the crumpled balls from the bag, opens them up, and shows the spectators that he had indeed written down each of the items they had thought of.

FURTHER READING

Barnhart, Norm. *Amazing Magic Tricks.* Mankato, MN: Capstone Press, 2008.

Charney, Steve. *Amazing Tricks with Everyday Stuff.* Mankato, MN: Capstone Press, 2011.

Charney, Steve. *Incredible Tricks at the Dinner Table.* Mankato, MN: Capstone Press, 2011.

Klingel, Cynthia. *Magic Tricks.* Mankato, MN: Compass Point Books, 2002.

Longe, Bob. *Classic Magic Tricks.* New York, NY: Metro Books, 2002.

Tremaine, Jon. *Instant Magic.* Hauppauge, NY: Barron's Educational Series, 2009.

WEB SITES

For Web resources related to the subject of this book, go to: www.windmillbooks.com/weblinks and select this book's title.

GLOSSARY

audience (AH-dee-ints) A group of people who watch or listen to something.

morph (MORF) To change in shape or form.

pledge (PLEJ) A promise or agreement.

prior (PRY-ur) Before or ahead of.

spectator (SPEK-tay-ter) A person who sees or watches something.

wiggles (WIH-gels) Makes small movements.

INDEX

A
assistant, 29, 31
audience, 4–5, 18–19, 26

B
bag, 24–25, 29–31

C
crease, 6–7, 22
cup, 12–13

N
newspaper, 9–11, 16

S
scissors, 11, 16, 24

T
tape, 9–11, 14, 22

WARMACHINE

RETRIBUTION OF SCYRAH

CREDITS

Creators of the Iron Kingdoms
Brian Snoddy
Matt Wilson

Chief Creative Officer
Matt Wilson

Project Director
Bryan Cutler

Game Design
Matt Wilson

Lead Developer
Jason Soles

Art Direction
Kris Aubin

Lead Writer
Douglas Seacat

Painting Guide Writer
Matt DiPietro

Continuity
Jason Soles

Editing
Darla Kennerud

Cover Illustration
Andrea Uderzo

Illustrations
Emrah Elmasli
Jeremy Jarvis
Torstein Nordstrand
Karl Richardson
Neil Roberts
Brian Snoddy
Andrea Uderzo
Chris Walton
Matt Wilson

Concept Illustration
Chris Walton
Matt Wilson

Graphic Design & Layout
Kris Aubin
Kim Goddard
Josh Manderville
Stuart Spengler

Studio Director
Ron Kruzie

Miniature Sculpting
Brian Dugas
Jeff Grace
Werner Klocke
Ben Misenar
Neil Roberts
Steve Saunders

Resin Caster
Sean Bullough

Miniature Painting
Matt DiPietro

Terrain
Rob Hawkins

Photography
Kris Aubin
Matt DiPietro
Rob Hawkins

Glyph Type Design
Arthur Braune
Chippy

Development Manager
Erik-Jason Yaple

Development
David Carl
Michael Faciane

Hobby Manager
Rob Hawkins

Product Line Coordinator
Rob Stoddard

Project Manager
Ed Bourelle

President
Sherry Yeary

Executive Assistant
Chare Kerzman

Marketing Coordinator
William Shick

Customer Service
Adam Johnson
Adam Poirier

Convention Coordinator
Dave Dauterive

Events Coordinator
Kevin Clark

Volunteer Coordinator
Dan Brandt

NQM EIC
Eric Cagle

Licensing & Contract Manager
Brent Waldher

Production Director
Mark Christensen

Technical Director
Kelly Yeager

Production Manager
Doug Colton

Production
Trey Alley
Max Barsana
Simon Berman
Alex Chobot
Jack Coleman
Joel Falkenhagen
Joe Lee
Mike McIntosh
Jacob Stanley
Ben Tracy
Clint Whiteside

Web Developer
Daryl Roberts

Infernals
Jeremy Galeone
Peter Gaublomme
Brian Putnam
Gilles Reynaud
John Simon
Donald Sullivan

Playtest Coordinator
David Carl

Playtesters
Greg Anecito
Kris Aubin
Alex Badion
Ed Bourelle
Dan Brandt
David Carl
Kevin Clark
Jack Coleman
Dave Dauterive
Michael Faciane
Joel Falkenhagen
Rob Hawkins
Adam Poirier
Brian Putnam
Douglas Seacat
William Shick
Jason Soles
Rob Stoddard
Chris Walton
Erik-Jason Yaple

Proofreading
Ed Bourelle
Alex Chobot
David Carl
David Dauterive
Darla Kennerud
Douglas Seacat
Jason Soles
Rob Stoddard

RETRIBUTION DAWNING

FACTION BACKGROUND

The nation of Ios has long isolated itself from the nations of the Iron Kingdoms. Among the few willing to venture outside its borders were members of the Retribution of Scyrah, a zealous and outlawed splinter sect devoted to stopping the proliferation of human magic. Recently, however, news that the Iosan god Nyssor is held captive in Khador stoked the embers of violence into a roaring flame set to consume the nations of man. Now those who support the Retribution's cause hold power in Ios, and their collected armies march forth to war.

Members of numerous Iosan houses have banded together at this turning point in history to fight for the future of their gods, their nation, and their entire race. This great army relies upon millennia of military tradition, the tactical acumen of their commanders, and the knowledge that should they fail there will be no tomorrow.

Myrmidons, the warjacks of Ios, are an enigma to the nations of the Iron Kingdoms. These sleek machines utilize technology far beyond the ken of man and march to war protected by shrouds of magical energy. On the field of battle, enemy soldiers quickly learn that the same energy that shields the myrmidons can be fired in powerful bursts of force.

PLAYING THE RETRIBUTION

Retribution armies are defined by their versatility. You can combine quick strikes from mage hunters with the hard-hitting power of Dawnguard, or you can focus on building a theme force of your favorite element. An entire army of Dawnguard is both striking to see and fun to play.

Myrmidons also have exceptional versatility and can shift their roles as needed. They can use their focus to regenerate their arcantrik fields or for model-specific boosts that allow the myrmidons to fulfill specialized roles. These myrmidons are supported by plentiful 'jack marshals and mechanics and work in impressive coordination with the warriors of the Retribution.

Armed with the might of the Retribution—the elusive Mage Hunters, the indomitable Dawnguard, the mystical Battle Mages, and the magic-fueled Myrmidons—you will soon see your enemies fall before the vengeful wrath of the Retribution of Scyrah. Show no mercy and take no surrender. After all . . .

They were warned.

TABLE OF CONTENTS

PRELUDE TO WAR 4

THE LONG FALL:
HISTORY OF IOS 22

MILITARY OF IOS
AND THE RETRIBUTION
OF SCYRAH 38

RETRIBUTION RULES 52

MODEL ENTRIES 56

PAINTING GUIDE 102

MODEL GALLERY 110

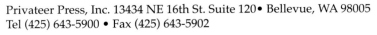

Visit: www.privateerpress.com

Privateer Press, Inc. 13434 NE 16th St. Suite 120• Bellevue, WA 98005
Tel (425) 643-5900 • Fax (425) 643-5902

For online customer service, email frontdesk@privateerpress.com

Fourth printing: June 2012. Printed in China.

Forces of WARMACHINE:
Retribution of Scyrah . . . . ISBN: 978-1-933362-48-9 . . . . PIP 1019

Forces of WARMACHINE:
Retribution of Scyrah Hardcover . . . . ISBN: 978-1-933362-49-6 . . . . PIP 1020

PRELUDE TO WAR

BLOOD TOLL

NORTHEAST OF CHEROV-ON-DRON, KHADOR

The two Khadoran sentries stood their post in companionable silence. They stared out from the wooden watchtower, bundled in heavy coats against the bitter cold. Spring was a meaningless season this far north of the Bitterrock River. The mood in the tower was worsened by the indistinct sounds of revelry from the barracks behind and below the tower. The 3rd Force had returned from Porsk bringing several bottles of a locally distilled *uiske*. While the sentries watched the frozen darkness, the others enjoyed a warm room, drinks, and laughter.

The barracks adjoined a cluster of other buildings within a low perimeter wall, serving collectively as a regional Khadoran kommand post. None of the soldiers knew much of the business conducted in these guarded military offices, except that it generated a great deal of paperwork and frequent visits by anxious and tight-lipped couriers. Most were of the opinion their superior officers handled essential but tedious tasks such as calculating military payrolls and staffing.

"Nigolev . . ." The younger of the two sentries broke the silence. "Do you ever regret being sent here rather than the front?"

The older Winter Guardsman shrugged. "Safer here. Better bored than dead, I say. Those stuck in the Thornwood would envy us."

"Maybe," he answered wistfully. "Nothing ever happens here. What is the point of having us here, in the middle of nowhere?"

"It is not our place to decide where we serve. Some soldiers go to fight and die in the mud. Others stand watch at quiet kommand posts and sleep in comfortable beds. Your young wife is happy you are here, yes?" He leered.

The younger man sighed. "I don't know. Sometimes I think she would rather I were not underfoot. Maybe she'd like it better with me hundreds of miles away, writing letters."

"Bah! If you were far away she would be weeping every night, worrying. 'Where is Sirov?' she would cry. I would have to comfort her. Trust me, it is better this way."

Nigolev chuckled at the glare he received until he heard a dull thump and felt a tremor in the wood where his arm was resting. He looked down in surprise at a quivering crossbow bolt lodged in the rail. His hand was already on his rifle before he fully realized they were under attack. "Sirov—" his warning was cut short as another bolt took him in the throat. He staggered back with a wet, gasping choke and fell to the floor.

Sirov's mouth dropped open and his eyes widened in horror. He turned and reached toward the long horn hanging on a strap from a hook at one corner of the tower. If he had simply hunkered down below the rail he might have lived longer, but his sense of duty compelled him to try to raise the alarm. A bolt sank into his shoulder even as he took the horn. Another bolt hit just below and to the left of the first, plunging through the thick jacket and the uniform beneath to pierce his lung. He slid down against the wall, still struggling to bring the horn to his lips. When he tried to sound it, his mouth filled with blood rather than air.

Several silhouettes emerged from the darkness to converge on the closed gate. One scrambled rapidly up and over the wall, a cloak covering his head and features, to open the gate for the rest from the other side. From within the nearby barracks the sounds of carousing continued, the volume of drunken mirth rising and falling like a tide.

The solemn figures advancing into the compound moved with smooth and professional economy as they took stock of their surroundings. Those fanning out ahead to the left and right communicated by sharp gestures and then dissolved into the darkness to stand ready. Several had pulled back their hoods to improve their vision, and their long and pointed ears revealed them to be Iosans. They were clad in heavy, dark leathers and were armed with blades at their hips in addition to crossbows in hand.

Their leader wore elaborately plated armor enameled in creamy white covering his upper torso and arms. Green-blue rune lines glowed at the joins of the large pauldron covering his left shoulder, and on his back a sleek exhaust vent protruded from a compact arcanik engine. He held a pair of elegant but unusual pistols, the grips of which were engineered with wicked backward-swept curved blades, each almost three feet in length. His hair was white and his face was gaunt and lined, suggesting his years had not been kind.

One of the nearby hunters fell back to him. This was a seasoned Iosan; his left cheek was puckered by thick scar tissue and his left ear was almost shorn off, remnants of old injuries. He spoke in a low tone. "Sentries are down, Garryth. We believe the target is in that building." He jerked his head over his shoulder to indicate the one building in the compound that resembled a traditional Khadoran townhouse. The windows were shuttered, but light glimmered from at least one of the lower rooms. It was the only other structure in the compound that showed signs of occupation. "What about the garrison?"

"They can't be left at our backs." He spoke softly, his expression unyielding. "We can't risk an interruption during the interrogation." Garryth was not in the habit of explaining his actions to subordinates, but he had sympathy for Commander Jarsyn, who had been operating out of a remote cell near Cherov-on-Dron for decades with little support. These men were accustomed to focusing more on covering their tracks than dealing substantial damage to the enemy. That was about to change.

Signaling to the mage hunters farther ahead, Garryth held up two fingers, then pointed first at his eyes and then at the townhouse. They nodded and moved ahead, positioning themselves to keep watch on that building. The warcaster turned and signaled to another Iosan lingering near the shadowed barracks wall. The heavily tattooed elf approached, his head cocked strangely to the side as he awaited instruction. He was close enough that his entirely black eyes were obvious, the mark of a soulless. Jarsyn's lip twitched and his nostrils flared in disgust as the soulless stepped closer to him. Garryth showed no discomfort.

"Nayl, enter the back as I take the front. Leave no one alive inside."

Nayl's expression was blank, his only sign of assent lifting his blade to ready position before heading to the rear of the barracks as instructed. Garryth sometimes felt alone in his appreciation for the way soulless could undertake any task without asking tedious questions. He turned back to the commander. "Give me a 15 count, then follow."

After waiting just long enough for Nayl to get into position, Garryth kicked open the front door and stepped inside. The drunken commotion did not immediately quiet, but many of the soldiers at the table nearest the door turned with stupefied expressions at the baffling sight of an elf in warcaster armor holding bladed pistols in hand. It was a long barracks hall, although occupied only to half capacity, with bunks lining each wall and tables down the center. Several guardsmen were in their bunks trying to sleep despite the noise, while most of the rest were clustered around the tables drinking and talking. Their short-hafted axes and blunderbusses were stowed close to hand in racks evenly spaced along the bunk rows.

Garryth did not give them the chance to think. He took several long strides into the room to reach the nearest table. As the shocked Khadorans lumbered to their feet he swept his bladed pistols in silver-glinting arcs, opening horrendous gaping wounds and sending men sprawling to die bleeding on the cold stone floor. He leapt across the table and with a downward slashing motion pinned two others to the wood near their spilled clay steins before jerking the weapons loose.

IOSAN FIREARMS

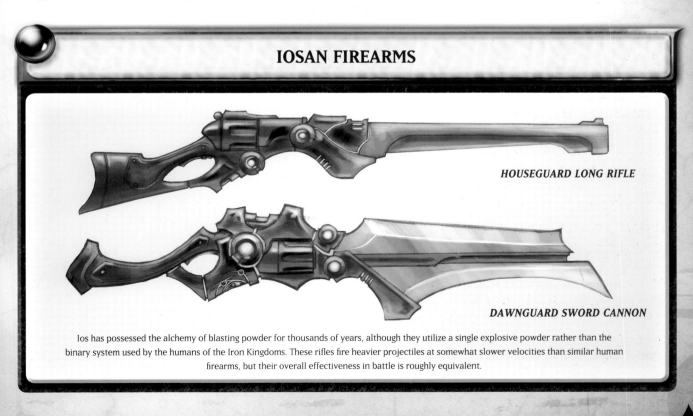

HOUSEGUARD LONG RIFLE

DAWNGUARD SWORD CANNON

Ios has possessed the alchemy of blasting powder for thousands of years, although they utilize a single explosive powder rather than the binary system used by the humans of the Iron Kingdoms. These rifles fire heavier projectiles at somewhat slower velocities than similar human firearms, but their overall effectiveness in battle is roughly equivalent.

At the far sides of the table two others managed to gather their wits enough to reach for nearby axes. Garryth impaled one of them before he could pull a weapon free and nimbly stepped to the side to evade the awkward swing of the second. He cut that man's throat with an almost casual backhanded slash as he moved to the second table. The Winter Guard seated there were in full panic, knocking one another aside in an attempt to get away from him. One particularly drunk man fell to his knees with his hands spread open and begged for his life. Garryth dispatched him with a quick flick of his blade without even looking at his face.

> "THIS IS THE ONLY PROMISE
> I WILL MAKE: IF YOU DO
> NOT ANSWER MY QUESTIONS,
> EVERYONE YOU LOVE WILL DIE."

With their attention on the bloodthirsty warcaster, the besotted soldiers failed to notice Nayl slip in the door at the back and move swiftly up behind those to the rear. His sword began to take its own toll. Several guardsmen managed to seize their blunderbusses, but it availed them little. Trembling fingers fumbled at loading the weapons, and in the end not a single shot was fired. Those who made it to their axes fared marginally better but met the same end. By the time the other hunters entered the hall there were only a few Winter Guard left living. There was a certain gleam of grim amusement and satisfaction in Garryth's eyes as he nodded approval to his team. He left the carnage behind him to advance on the townhouse.

The Greylord sat lashed to the chair in his lower laboratory, looking from one Iosan face to the next. Despite his evident fear there was defiance in his gritted teeth and the way his hands clenched the ropes behind his back. He was still straining against his confines rather than slumping in defeat. His freezing magic had taken the life of one of the junior hunters, whose body others had hauled away to be properly disposed of later.

The room was littered with books and arcane paraphernalia, including a small but expensive private alchemy laboratory in the far corner and what looked to be a costly inlaid-silver mystic diagram covering much of the floor. Garryth stood in front of the captive and Nayl behind him, the soulless' face lost to shadow.

"Why should I tell you anything?" the Khadoran snarled. He spewed a gobbet of blood that missed Garryth to spatter onto the floor. All those present understood the Khadoran tongue, having learned the simple languages of their enemies as a necessity of their work.

Garryth spat his response as if the Khadoran words left a bad taste in his mouth. "I am not here to torture you, although there are those among us who could force you to speak. I am sure you would hold out for a time. Perhaps you would enjoy the pain. No. I will also not promise to spare your life. Koldun Vorezko Makovich is a dead man."

The Greylord's eyes widened as he stared at the Iosan, clearly baffled. At this base he worked under an alias fabricated to obscure his identity. "How—"

"Yes, I know you. You report to Fedor Rachlavsky, the head of your Prikaz Chancellery. You investigate irregularities in the funding of Greylord Covenant operations. Your wife is named Senya, and she recently gave birth to your third child, a son. Do you want me to describe the house in Porsk where you thought they were safe?"

The blood in the koldun's face drained away, leaving him pale and shaking. Garryth smiled maliciously. The Khadoran stuttered, "No . . . You cannot . . ."

"She is unharmed—for now." He paused, watching hope rekindle in the Khadoran's eyes. "This is the only promise I will make: If you do not answer my questions, everyone you love will die. If you answer, they will be spared. I will forgive for now the taint of sorcery polluting their veins. Try to keep my attention elsewhere, Makovich." His eyes bored into the Greylord's, who shuddered and looked away, gasping.

"What do you want to know?" Now he slumped, as if his vitality had been stolen away.

"You are investigating a woman of your order, Koldun Kommander Aleksandra Zerkova. She has placed a burden on your carefully balanced budgets. Tell me where she has been spending this coin. Satisfy me and you die in peace. I will forget about your wife and children."

Words spilled from the prisoner in a torrent. A man of his word, Garryth rewarded him with a quick and relatively merciful end.

As the Iosan wiped his blade clean, he saw Nayl approach the body. The black eyes of the soulless stared fixedly at the dead koldun. Garryth had seen this before. If left to his own devices, Nayl would crudely dissect the man and extract his organs to examine them with impartial curiosity. "Stop," he ordered. The soulless paused and turned to him, his head tilted like an inquisitive hound's. The warcaster asked, "Why do you do that?"

Nayl answered in his strangely uninflected voice, "I am looking for what makes them different."

Garryth seemed amused. "What have you found?"

The soulless shook his head. "Nothing. They seem almost identical to us, anatomically."

Garryth laughed in morbid humor. "We have no time for such foolishness. You'll have another chance soon enough." He turned to Commander Jarsyn. "I will return to Ios while you prepare your teams here. I have what we need." He glanced around at the piles of carefully organized books and papers. After waving the others out of the room, he knocked a nearby oil lantern onto its side and watched as the fire quickly spread. Garryth's eyes reflected calm serenity. His expression conveyed the absolute peace of a man who had delivered righteous vengeance in the name of his goddess.

THE GODDESS STIRS

INNER FANE, SHYRR, IOS

The bustle of preparations elsewhere, the mustering of soldiers gearing up for march, the deep thrum of myrmidons powering their fields, the heavy tread of steps on pavement—none of these intruded on the quiet sanctity of the inner chamber below the fane in Shyrr. In this place there was only meditative peace and tranquility. A living stillness permeated the calm of the divine bedchamber it was.

In many aspects the room resembled a tomb. All its surfaces were stone, with rising columns inscribed in gleaming metal sigils supporting the ceiling. Even the elevated platform where the goddess rested seemed more a bier than a bed, with its simple stone slab lacking even the simple creature comforts of cushions or blankets. Lying sheathed on the highest step beside this platform rested *Telmirr*, the holy sword whose name meant "Winter's End." An occasional faint shimmer of green vibrancy flickered across its sheath, its hilt, and its oval pommel.

The armored knight kneeling in vigil before the platform remembered the first time he had come to this place. This was the highest honor of his order: the opportunity to personally protect the goddess and thereby stand in the Presence. The room's stark simplicity had startled him. It had seemed a cruelty to let the ailing goddess languish on cold stone adorned only in her gossamer gown. The attending priests insisted this was how the gods had always rested, even when they had been eight in number and active participants in their communities. Stone was no discomfort to them; their divine flesh had no need of the luxuries taken for granted by even the poorest of Ios' citizens.

In the last two years Fane Knight Skeryth Issyen had become increasingly fond of the chamber, until now it was the one place he felt entirely at peace. The room was filled with warmth that seemed to radiate from Scyrah herself. If he stood still and completely quiet, he could hear the soft and regular exhalations of the goddess' breath. The lighting in the room was subdued, but he could clearly see her slender form in rest. Sometimes she would turn in her sleep to face toward him, and his world would freeze as he beheld the sublime perfection of her features. He felt compelled at such times to avert his gaze, once he could gather the wits to do so.

This night even the Presence could not ease his inner turmoil. It would be his last vigil. Increasingly his mind returned to the decision he had made, wondering if he had chosen rightly. But how could he stay here watching while her life slipped invisibly away? If they did not act this chamber would become the tomb it had first resembled to him. All of Ios would crumble to ruin and be forgotten, unless Scyrah could be saved. He must hold onto the hope that something could avert the fate that the fane priests accepted as inevitable.

It felt a blasphemy to speak, but he could not restrain himself. If these were to be his final minutes in the Presence, he had to ask. His heart beating rapidly in his chest, he whispered, "Have I chosen well? Is war the right solution?"

He did not expect anything resembling a response. His breath caught as Scyrah turned in her slumber and the soft flow of her hair tumbled off the side of the stone like the finest spun gold. Several strands came to rest upon the hilt of Telmirr. Her eyes remained closed, but her lips moved as if in speech and he took a step closer, straining to hear. Even in the silence of the chamber it was difficult to discern the words, but he thought he heard, ". . . some leaves must fall."

It was a frozen moment of timeless wonder until spots before Skeryth's eyes reminded him to breathe. He realized the indecorum of having stepped closer and quickly drew back while his heart beat painfully. He heard footsteps behind him and turned to see the robed form of Auricant Avross Larisar in the doorway. The older priest spoke softly. "It is time."

Skeryth Issyen forced his legs to obey and turned away from the goddess, knowing he would likely never behold her again. This grief was tempered by the fresh exultation of having received an undeniable sign. He remained lost in thought and almost forgot the priest until they reached the outer entrance to the inner fane, at which point Avross stopped and said, "I wish you well, Skeryth Issyen. I will not try again to dissuade you. I know your mind is decided. I only hope this does not prove to be a mistake."

The fane knight bowed deeply. "I appreciate your concerns, Auricant. As promised, I will keep you apprised as to what transpires while I am abroad."

"Please do." He paused a moment and added, "You should know that, of all of them, you can put your trust in Ravyn. Her heart and faith are true. She awaits you now, outside. I will pray for both of you." The priest withdrew and the massive doors closed silently, leaving no visible seam.

Skeryth pondered those words as he walked away, passing through several long and cool corridors and guarded archways until he reached the stairs ascending to the surface. Despite the rumors that Auricant Avross harbored Retribution sympathies, for a man in his position to speak so highly of a former outcast like Ravyn was telling. She had not been welcome in the Fane of Scyrah since abandoning her vows. Her presence now on fane grounds was a sign of how much things had changed in just a few months.

He spotted her as he exited the main doors of the great fane. She stood just down the path within the perfectly ordered garden that surrounded the colossal stones of the central worship structure. Seeing his approach, Ravyn greeted him with a smile, but her expression was strained. She had at one time been his superior among the Fane Knights before she had felt compelled by her conscience to leave and join the Retribution. Her hair was as black as her namesake, with a single long streak of solid white, which gave her slender features a commanding air despite her youth. Not that she was as young as she appeared to be, Skeryth reminded himself; he was several decades her junior.

She was still young for being thrust into such a significant position of leadership within the Retribution of Scyrah. The Nine Voices, its ruling council, called Ravyn the "Eternal Light." This appellation was a sign of their faith in her, but it also represented a burden of responsibility. She was entrusted to represent them abroad, leading their forces to war outside Ios. Earlier in the month she had offered him a choice that would forever change his life.

> ## "WE RECEIVED NEWS OF NYSSOR'S LIKELY LOCATION. WINTER'S HAMMER IS IN MOTION."

It was notable that she not only wore her warcaster armor but also carried Hellebore, her halberd-cannon, strapped to her back. A few months ago she might have been arrested for stepping on fane grounds even as a humble supplicant, yet here she was armed for battle. Skeryth did see several members of his order watching tensely from a discreet distance. It would take more than a pronouncement of amnesty from the Consulate Court before many people would trust known members of the Retribution, even those as famous and widely regarded as Ravyn.

"How many years has it been since I stood here?" Ravyn said as he drew close. She immediately shook her head, as if annoyed at her own sentimental urges. "Never mind. It doesn't matter now." She turned to face him more squarely, and her voice adopted a more commanding tone. "I hope your affairs are in order. There is no time to waste. The last of our forces are ready to march. I told them I would rejoin them as soon as I had collected you."

Skeryth had not intended to speak on the topic, but the words emerged of their own accord. "Ravyn, I just received a sign from the goddess." His voice carried the urgency he felt in his blood. "She endorses this action. Our mission. I am certain of it." Even saying this much was technically a violation of his vows, but Skeryth could not restrain his enthusiasm.

He could see the fire of hope kindle in her eyes. "Praise the Goddess!" She knew better than to ask for additional details. What transpired during the vigil of a Fane Knight was sacrosanct. She mused under her breath, "All the pieces fall into place . . ." At his quizzical expression she clarified, "While you were at your vigil we received news of Nyssor's likely location. Winter's Hammer is in motion. That is why I am here. I need you to prepare your steed and meet me at the Horned Arch. We will hurry to catch up with the others. We muster at the Gate of Mists."

He asked, "Why did you wait for me? You could have sent word."

She smiled. "I knew it would be harder for you to change your mind if I was here in person." She ignored his indignant expression and admonished more seriously, "Know this. I will not let you stand idly while my men fight and die. Whatever the priests instructed you, we do not need an 'observer.' When the battle begins, I expect your support."

"I will fight. You have my word." At this he offered a respectful bow and took his leave. He made his way to the path to the stables, ignoring numerous glares from others wearing Scyrah's symbol. Confused by his decision to march alongside Ravyn and the Retribution, his peers no longer considered him a brother. For once this did not trouble him. His choice was made.

"You are late." Adeptis Rahn Shyeel's voice was sardonic but not actually angry. There were chairs around the map-strewn table at the center of the room but both he and the other occupant of the room were standing. The senior-most battle mage of House Shyeel was only partially attired in his war gear, wearing only a few pieces of his formidable armor.

Ravyn ignored the light reprimand and offered respectful nods to both the adeptis and Dawnlord Vyros Nyarr. The latter was leaning over the table scowling at the maps before him. He also was not yet geared for battle, although both men conveyed the impression they could be ready at a moment's notice. Even lacking the full regalia of his Dawnguard armor, Vyros Nyarr was an imposing man whose stern glare could silence even members of the Consulate Court. Ravyn knew she would be working closely alongside the dawnlord and refused to let his reputation intimidate her. Her nod to him was that of one equal to another. "It looks like your preparations are well in hand. The speed with which you have mobilized is impressive."

Dawnlord Vyros' slight smile conveyed his sense of satisfaction. He affirmed, "We have been preparing for months. All we needed was a target." His red-tailed hawk screeched from its post behind him in the corner, where her talons clutched the wood. She was unhooded and shook her wings as if eager to hunt.

Ravyn had ridden hard from Shyrr to reach the Gate of Mists in just seven days. On her arrival she witnessed ordered regiments of thousands of eager soldiers alongside dozens of House Shyeel myrmidons. These forces had taken over the fortress' reserve barracks, requiring unusual accommodations from House Rhyslyrr, the Great House controlling this vital gate. She had seen the naked hostility with which Homeguard Coalition soldiers treated their Retribution counterparts.

Arranging this force so quickly had been a logistical nightmare, yet the Dawnguard officers acted with impressive precision. Everyone knew the stakes, both for their mission and for the Retribution itself. This would be the hour to prove they could function as a cohesive army. It was a demonstration of strength and efficiency to the other Iosan houses.

Adeptis Rahn turned to Ravyn with evident curiosity, crossing his arms and looking her up and down as if assessing a novice of his house. Until recently they had experienced very little direct interaction. "Were you delayed by coddling that knight from House Issyen? He is just one man."

Only her narrowed eyebrows conveyed her irritation. "He will be an important symbol. His joining us will create many ripples, Adeptis."

"So you say." His eyes were unyielding. The adeptis managed to convey a sense of weight with even the smallest of gestures or expressions. It was as if he were always restraining impulses to unleash his mental powers and crush whomever he was addressing.

Ravyn tore her eyes away to continue, "My people are ready for their part. Garryth will join your task force directly, Adeptis. His teams will assist you in whatever capacity your plans require."

"My *plans* will likely change the moment we encounter the enemy," Rahn insisted. Despite his petulant tone the mention of Garryth's name obviously satisfied him, as Ravyn had hoped. Garryth's long record of accomplishment

IOSAN HALBERD

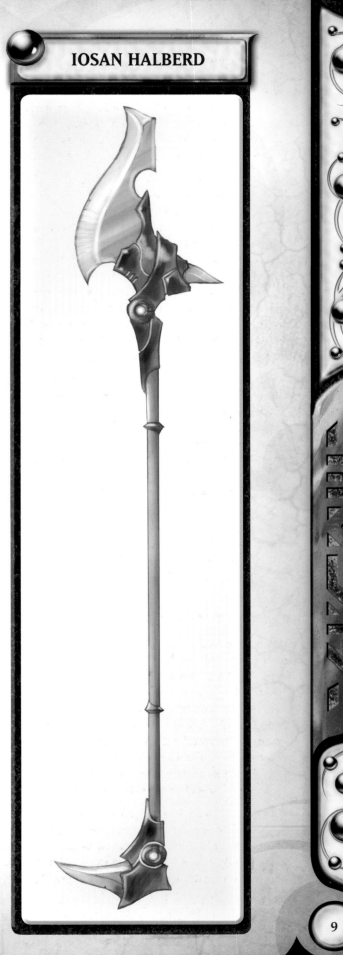

was well known to all of them, and she had anticipated that the adeptis and the Blade of Retribution might form an effective tactical pairing.

"Attend me." Dawnlord Vyros' deep voice commanded their attention as he pointed to the map. "We must prepare additional contingencies in case the Khadorans do not react as predicted to Barbed Thorn." Ravyn came closer to examine the complicated marks on the map in front of him.

Rahn's stiff posture suggested mild affront. "Rest assured, Vyros: I will give them no choice. They will give chase."

> THEIR MASSIVE GRENADE—TIPPED ARROWS SOARED IN A HIGH ARC ACROSS THE INTERVENING DARKNESS TO IMPACT AND EXPLODE INTO A WALL OF FIRE

PRODDING THE BEAR

EAST OF LAEDRY, OCCUPIED LLAEL

Adeptis Rahn Shyeel let his arm fall, and the line of Stormfall archers lifted their compound bows in unison and let fly. Their massive grenade-tipped arrows soared in a high arc across the intervening darkness to impact and explode into a wall of fire that erupted across the roofs and tents of the garrisoned force east of Laedry. Garryth had been as good as his word, and no sentry or perimeter patrol had survived to forewarn them of the imminent attack.

Khadorans came pouring out of the burning buildings into the din of shouted orders and queries. Soldiers rushed frantically in every direction, while commanding sergeants and officers tried to call them into line. Gunfire in their midst dropped a number of them, but the chaos settled with surprising speed.

The Khadoran response proved to be more cool-headed than the Shyeel adeptis had hoped for. Perhaps it was to be expected, given that these men had experience dealing with an unruly populace and outbreaks of violence. The soldiers quickly hunkered down into the trenchworks and low, defensive walls surrounding the building to fire crude short-barreled firearms into the darkness, perhaps hoping to suppress whatever enemy attacked them on this miserably overcast night. Even the moons were hidden this evening, and the poor visibility was worsened by the fire and smoke. The Khadorans' shots were nowhere near the mark, but the soldiers' battle fitness after being roused from sleep by fire remained commendable.

While some Winter Guard dealt with the fires, Rahn saw other men hauling heavier ordinance into position, including field guns and mortars. Farther back he could see the silhouettes of several lumbering Khadoran heavy warjacks moving up to support the entrenched positions. These machines must have been kept fired and idling as a precaution against unexpected attacks.

"Perhaps they mean to give us a real fight after all," he mused aloud to his nearest senior officers. These included Shyeel Battle Mage Magister Nyven and Thane Lyvenne, commander of Rahn's Houseguard Riflemen. The latter stood with her soldiers lined up along the ridge in good firing positions. Both the riflemen and the Stormfall archers wore goggles designed to enhance vision in low-light conditions. Such devices were inferior to natural daylight but provided them an advantage over the nearly blind Khadorans.

Rahn wore no goggles, but the darkness did not bother him. He had other means to extend his senses. In addition to the enhanced perspective of seeing through the eyes of multiple myrmidons, he could sense the play of raw forces around him. The discharge of each rifle appeared as a blast of light to his arcane vision, while each projectile sent a rippling wake of kinetic force. The air in front of him was bright and alive with the traces of these violent patterns.

"If simple fire does not frighten them, let us show them something that will. Thane Lyvenne, prepare for full assault." She blinked in surprise at this departure from their plan of action but quickly conveyed his order down the line.

By mental command Rahn sent his myrmidons forward, including a Phoenix and two Hydras, flanked by a pair of Chimeras. A number of others waited not far from their position, held back as a reserve. Rahn did not expect he would need them, not tonight.

Even in the darkness the three heavy myrmidons shimmered with light as power collected and pooled in the energy fields surrounding them. The Hydras glowed brightly against the night's darkness as ripples collected in their fields and converged at their central firing lens apertures. Each circular crystalline nodule at the center of their armored torsos lit with blinding radiance as lances of energy fired through their respective fields, gathering power in a vortex that pulsed outward toward the distant enemy. Raw energy impacted into the Khadoran trenches, burning flesh from bones where they struck.

The Phoenix's attack sequence was even more dramatic, as its field was limned with bluish-green fire that launched like a shrieking bird of prey to explode into the midst of the Winter Guard. Several were killed on impact, while the unnatural fire blazed across the fallen and lit alight several nearby soldiers, who ran and fell screaming.

It was the Khadorans' first taste of myrmidon firepower, the first clue they were not facing armed insurgents or other familiar enemies. Adeptis Rahn took delight in the naked fear on the faces illuminated by the blaze.

The Khadoran heavies ran forward. There was a dull thump as a bombard sent its shell toward the attackers. A chorus of other thumps preceded the screeching of incoming fire as the rain of mortar shells began to fall. Rahn saw these incoming projectiles with his force-sensitive vision and disdainfully sent a wave of mental energy to deflect them, letting them fall well short of his forward line. His Hydras and the Phoenix continued to fire as they closed the gap. Rahn signaled his halberdiers, riflemen, and subordinate battle mages to press forward. The riflemen stopped periodically to fire before resuming their advance, while the battle mages sent rippling waves of concentrated force to tear apart the Khadoran soldiers.

"Nicely done." said a voice to Rahn's left. He did not visibly startle, but Garryth's proximity unnerved him for a moment. Mage hunter warcasters learned to dampen outward manifestations of their power, but it was a knack few could manage against someone as sensitive as the adeptis, who could normally perceive other warcasters at a considerable distance. No matter how alert Rahn believed himself to be, Garryth always found a way to approach him unawares, perhaps as some sort of private sport. Garryth's voice carried a hint of dry humor as he observed, "This does not look like a withdrawal."

"On evaluating our plan I came to the conclusion that picking a fight and fleeing would not represent us as a credible threat." For a man of Rahn's ability, maintaining control over so many advancing myrmidons while carrying on a conversation was not difficult.

As he spoke, the Hydra on the far left converged on the Khadoran Destroyer, its fists aglow with emerald light as it shook the hull with punishing blows. The Khadoran armor was thick and weathered this onslaught well, but the machine was forced to stagger backward with each impact. When the Destroyer started to falter on its cruder piston-driven legs, the Hydra seized it and flung it backward into the nearest wall, which exploded into a cloud of brick and dust.

Rahn continued without pause, "For our gambit to work they must feel endangered. We will raze this barracks and hold until reinforcements arrive." Rahn's gauntlet hummed and began to vibrate and glow with bright green-blue light. The very stones around his feet rose and gleamed as gravity was negated by ripples of concentrated force, which he then released with a sudden thrust of his hand toward the farthest Chimera. Its arc node vents blazed as this power flowed through them to explode with raw force into a mortar emplacement, tearing it apart with a metallic protest. A secondary explosion of chaotic torque tore several men limb from limb as they were trying to extinguish a fire behind the mortar team. When Rahn spoke again, the light tone in his voice contrasted with the violence. "This is, after all, only one of six major reserves near Laedry. When they commit against us, we will pull back to the mountains."

Garryth grinned coldly at the adeptis. "I like the way you think." He raised his bladed pistols and broke away toward the Khadorans on his left, his myrmidons mirroring his movements. Garryth fired on targets of opportunity as he closed while several groups of mage hunters followed suit, making efficient use of their crossbows.

COLD STORAGE

NEAR FORT BRUNZIG, KHADOR

Kommander Alexandra Zerkova stood silently in the freezing underground chamber. Her senior aid stood by her side, reading aloud the day's dispatches, but she did not seem to be listening. She stared with her one good eye at the rune-laden stone vault in front of her as if she could force it to divulge its secrets through sheer force of will. Elevated upon a small stand near the vault and held in place by several black metal clamps was the Torch of Lord Khazarak. It was the artifact the eldritch Goreshade had employed during his attack in the Korsk cathedral to melt the solid block of ice within the vault. It had resisted all Zerkova's attempts to reignite its flame.

Heavy lines beneath Zerkova's eyes suggested she had not been sleeping. There was a strained silence between her and the other Greylords working in the room. All attempts to breach the icy vault had failed. A variety of conductive metal plates, thick piping, and flexible tubes were arrayed around and connected to the object of their study. The one task they had succeeded at was harnessing the tremendous supernatural cold pouring from this object. Zerkova was convinced she was on the threshold of a greater discovery of profound significance, if only she could gain access to the interior.

The large room was choked with a bewildering array of mechanikal and occult apparatus as well as cruder tools such as massive hammers, chisels, and a large steam-driven drill. The forge taking up the entirety of the north

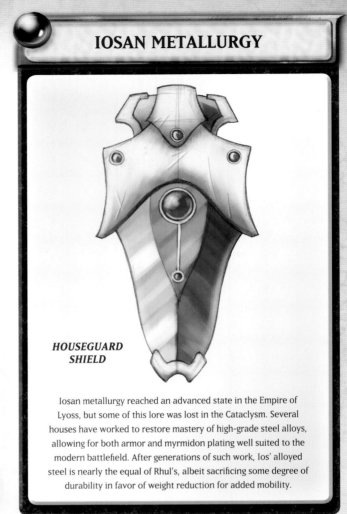

IOSAN METALLURGY

HOUSEGUARD SHIELD

Iosan metallurgy reached an advanced state in the Empire of Lyoss, but some of this lore was lost in the Cataclysm. Several houses have worked to restore mastery of high-grade steel alloys, allowing for both armor and myrmidon plating well suited to the modern battlefield. After generations of such work, Ios' alloyed steel is nearly the equal of Rhul's, albeit sacrificing some degree of durability in favor of weight reduction for added mobility.

wall did not much diminish the unnatural cold of the chamber, but its constant heat was the only reason they could function in the chamber at all. The temperatures were low enough to put even bundled Greylords skilled in ice magic at risk. One of the first ancillary researchers had frozen to death during his shift, after which Zerkova had imposed a strict schedule rotation. No one except Zerkova herself was allowed to work on the project for more than three hours at a time, and never alone.

Her subordinate finished his summation and stood uncomfortably in silence, waiting for a reaction. After several seconds she finally turned away from the vault with a frown. "Did you say Iosan attacks in Llael? Has this been confirmed?"

"Yes, Kommander, this report is genuine." He looked down at the dispatches. "Reliable witnesses independently confirmed several sizable attacks in western Llael. Iosan warjacks and warcasters were allegedly involved, most notably at an attack near Laedry. Several reserve garrisons are being ordered to join occupation forces in Llael. We may be next."

Zerkova took the papers from him, and her brow furrowed as she flipped through them. She was not one prone to conspiratorial thinking, but the described list of attacks made little sense from any conventional strategic perspective. After so long in isolation, why would Ios emerge to attack seemingly random targets and withdraw? Khadoran battalions were currently in pursuit, hoping to retaliate for their losses. To Zerkova this suggested they had been manipulated. The question remained: what did Ios hope to gain? The attacks were too remote to suggest any connection to her work, but she felt apprehensive. That their timing was so close to the surprise attack on Makovich's kommand post several months ago set off certain alarms in her mind. That man's death had been convenient, as he had been prying into her affairs, but its circumstances were still peculiar. There was no evidence that Iosans had been behind that attack, but Zerkova sensed certain tenuous threads connecting these events. Unexplained Greylord deaths were on the rise, and a conspiracy did not seem implausible.

Although Zerkova did not feel inclined to voice such thoughts to her subordinate, she saw no harm in prudence. "Tell the men to stay at high alert and to double all patrols." He nodded and left to do as bid, clearly eager to return to the warmer environs of the surface bunker.

Zerkova looked again at the frozen vault, considering that the time had come to set the final pieces of her evacuation contingency into place. Those arrangements had become a high priority when she had learned of Koldun Makovich's investigation, but certain details had been left unfixed to allow for flexibility. As reluctant as she was to take any time from the enigma of the Nyss vault, she decided to handle this personally. The fewer people involved, the better. Her time in the Covenant had taught her not to rely on the loyalty of others when self-preservation was at stake. She had risked much to secure this vault, keeping its particulars secret even from her own order. She would not chance its security.

STRENGTH FOR STRENGTH

NEAR FORT BRUNZIG, KHADOR

The Retribution army led by Dawnlord Vyros Nyarr was given only a brief chance to rest after more than a month of grueling travel. They had been marching as far as possible both night and day with only short breaks. Exhaustion had added to the tension of the constant fear of discovery and attack once they had violated Khador's border.

The march was difficult even for those who were caught up in the enthusiasm of being part of the first large-scale assault on foreign soil in Iosan history. Yet excitement lingered even in times of exhaustion, ready to ignite at the slightest

encouragement. Even the normally insular Dawnguard were not immune. An awareness of the scope of their task served as a catalyst for bonds to form between the varied members of the Winter's Hammer task force.

Mage hunters served as unseen guardians by keeping pace beyond the fringes of the marching army. They did not speak of how many they killed to preserve the secrecy of their mission, but the lack of a general alarm or the appearance of an opposing army suggested both they and the Barbed Thorn task force led by Adeptis Rahn were succeeding at their respective tasks. They had done the unimaginable by smuggling an entire army deep into the Khadoran heartland.

The path they had taken was deliberately circuitous, both to evade detection and to allow for periodic stops at Retribution strongholds previously established abroad. Of these, just the mustering point nearest their target was large enough to shelter the entire army, and they managed it there only by enduring barely livable accommodations.

The stronghold was an extensive network of underground caves and tunnels originally excavated for a mining project. The mine had been exhausted and then abandoned and forgotten by the Khadorans long ago. It suited the Retribution's needs quite well, being both hidden and extensive enough to hide soldiers and myrmidons. The Nine Voices and their secret backers had invested considerable funds in turning these excavations into a fully outfitted facility. Despite these efforts, it had never been intended to house so many, and all the officers knew finite supplies limited their time here. Still, even this brief rest provided a much-needed respite for their exhausted soldiers and allowed their myrmidons to recharge power reserves to full.

Kaelyssa felt great relief at two luxurious days standing relatively still in a single location, even if it did feel like they were confined to a prison. The underground nature of the complex meant she was able to give most members of her teams a break from their vigils, although a small number took turns keeping watch outside.

> THEY HAD DONE THE UNIMAGINABLE BY SMUGGLING AN ENTIRE ARMY DEEP INTO THE KHADORAN HEARTLAND.

At the moment she was enjoying a short interval of camaraderie with several of her strike team sergeants in the crowded confines of an oddly shaped chamber that had become an impromptu gathering spot. The room had an uncomfortably low ceiling and was too small to be a sleeping chamber. Seated on a variety of empty supply crates gathered to serve as chairs, the group passed a flask of fortified wine between them while swapping stories of previous missions. It was an attempt to clear their minds on the eve of battle.

The sergeants went suddenly silent and Kaelyssa saw them looking over her shoulder. She turned to see Ravyn entering the room. "Welcome, Ravyn." Kaelyssa's tongue felt a bit thick as she offered the wine flask.

As expected, her superior smiled but declined. The sergeants quickly found excuses to take their leave, mumbling polite formalities before slipping away. Ravyn possessed an undeniable mystique among the mage hunters, who revered her to the point they were uncomfortable in her presence. This had become particularly evident in the close confines of the underground base. Because of this, more often than not Ravyn was left to her own company.

"I did not mean to disrupt your time with your men," Ravyn offered by way of apology. "I thought we should talk before the battle."

Kaelyssa took another swallow of wine and smiled, feeling more at ease with this woman than she might have if she had not been drinking. "I've been meaning to ask you something. Do you really think this entire production is necessary? How much of what we are doing here is part of some political game between Nyarr and Shyeel?"

Ravyn blinked and seemed set back by the abrupt question. "What do you mean? Surely you do not doubt the importance of recovering Nyssor . . . ?"

Kaelyssa waved her hand in negation. "No, no. But why can't we do things *our* way? A few strike forces at night, in secret. A handful of myrmidons. Give me a few Chimeras and a Manticore. We break into the bunker, kill those who need killing, and free Nyssor. If he's even there. Why ready for open war? Seems like an excuse to let Vyros and his Dawnguard posture for glory. The fact that Garryth isn't even here is ridiculous—" She realized the wine had loosened her tongue too much when she saw the red rise in Ravyn's cheeks and her eyebrows narrowed into an angry scowl.

The senior warcaster retorted, "First of all, we might not have gotten here safely if Garryth had not been fighting elsewhere. Second, it is *Dawnlord* Vyros. I suggest you speak his name with respect, particularly if you ever expect to lead his men in battle." Ravyn abruptly stopped, perhaps realizing she was lecturing. She sighed and continued with less heat. "I understand your concerns, but this battle plan is necessary. It is no political show. I would never waste the lives of those entrusted to my care on empty symbolic gestures."

Kaelyssa felt slightly abashed. "I trust you, Ravyn. I do. But explain to me why the Dawnguard are here. A lot of our people are asking the same thing. I'm not convinced we need them."

Ravyn brushed her hair behind her ear as she sat down next to the younger warcaster. Kaelyssa was surprised at this friendly gesture and listened quietly as Ravyn stated her case. "I've examined the maps a dozen times. This will be a bloody fight regardless of our approach. Our diviners insist the Greylords have this bunker sealed and mystically warded. Its alarms are connected directly to Fort Brunzig, whose garrison was recently reinforced. Khadoran soldiers by the hundreds are being outfitted there before being rotated to the front lines. More troops can be brought in by rail on short notice."

"Fast in, fast out, then," Kaelyssa insisted, although she did not sound as certain.

Ravyn shook her head. "If we go in with a small group, we will trigger the alarms and be cut off and surrounded. The only way for this plan to work is to strike hard and seize the facility while the bulk of our forces are waiting to intercept the reinforcements we know will be sent from Brunzig. Even with the firepower at our disposal, this will be risky. Dawnlord Vyros and his men will take the brunt of the bloodiest fighting. They are our shield."

Kaelyssa pondered this explanation. "Fine. I'll take your word. But if those Nyarr prigs aren't where we need them when our back is against the wall, so help me . . . I am not above shooting Vyros' precious bird and cooking it for dinner."

This ridiculous image was enough to provoke startled laughter from the normally taciturn Ravyn. "On second thought, I will have some of that wine." She reached for the flask and took a measured swallow. On handing it back she gave Kaelyssa a serious look. "I will be supporting the Dawnguard tomorrow. You will lead the strike on the bunker. They will make you bleed at every step. Do your best, but above all I expect you to come out of this alive."

Kaelyssa offered a confident grin. "Leave it to me. We're ready."

Ravyn stood and put a hand on the other warcaster's shoulder. "I know. May Scyrah watch over you, Kaelyssa, Night's Whisper." She took her leave, and Kaelyssa looked after her with a puzzled expression, feeling inexplicably comforted, as if she had in fact been blessed.

Kaelyssa watched tensely from the nighttime darkness under a rock overhang that afforded a protected view of the upper bunker entrance. The area was gated off and patrolled, but her people had become well accustomed to the guards' movements.

This bunker had been just a dot of potential interest on Retribution maps before Garryth's mission, an oversight their local agents had spent the last month attempting to rectify. Gathering intelligence on the facility had been difficult, as the Greylord Aleksandra Zerkova had covered her tracks well. Fortunately active surveillance had served where other methods had failed.

There was a likely second route into the bunker via a short rail line that went underground just north of here and possibly extended to the underside of the facility. Its tunnel entrance was sealed off and seemed both neglected and unused, as surveillance had sighted no activity there in the last month. Two mage hunter teams kept watch just in case, but it was deemed the less useful point of ingress. This smaller surface entrance chosen for their mission was protected by an armored door and the adjoining thick-walled upper bunker. This included an observation chamber where several men could peer out through narrow slits at the only approaching path. The steel-reinforced bunker looked capable of enduring sustained cannon fire, particularly as the bulk of the facility was below ground. Breaching this entrance by force would not have been easily or quickly accomplished.

The timing of their mission depended on information only recently confirmed, and Kaelyssa felt the itch of uncertainty as time stretched on. It would be dawn soon. Already the sky was brightening in the east. At last they heard the approach of horses and a wagon on the trail, and soon the anticipated small resupply wagon passed their position. One of the horses caught their scent and whinnied in alarm, but the drivers ignored the beast and pushed on. Surveillance had shown that this wagon brought fresh food and drink to the bunker every week. It was late.

Her first team fell into line directly behind the wagon, using its shape to obscure themselves from any watching from inside the bunker. A patrol of two men on foot approached the wagon from the left, but in the blink of an eye they were gone, caught by mage hunters who dropped cloaks over their faces to pull them back and neatly slit their throats. The men driving the wagon saw nothing and continued, finally pulling to a stop on the flat, open area before the entrance.

The gas lanterns lighting the immediate entry left ample shadows, and the hunters moved like phantoms in the dimness. Those watching from the dome-like observation point saw only the wagon halted as usual in the pooled light before the entrance. From the metal door rasped the sound of securing rods being withdrawn, and it swung open to reveal a well-lit corridor extending down into the ground. A single soldier came forth to greet the wagon drivers and light a cigar. Two others climbed up from the bunker and moved around the sides to offload the supplies.

Kaelyssa gestured to her senior commander who nodded and quickly passed the signal. The hunter force swept forward as if of one mind, using blades to take down the soldiers and drivers quickly and then turning loaded crossbows toward the thick-walled observation post. The men within were barely visible by the silhouettes of their heads through the viewing slits. Before they could react to the sudden appearance of intruders multiple crossbows fired. Instead of shattering against the intervening bunker wall these bolts faded and vanished midflight. There was the satisfying sound of fleshy impacts within the domed chamber as the phantom seekers found their marks.

Kaelyssa was the first through the open door into the bunker. She immediately sped down the stairs, raising her runebolt cannon toward a cloaked figure she saw turn to flee. This man, wearing the robes of a Greylord, managed to reach a heavy lever and grasped it with both hands before she fired. He yanked it down just as her runebolt took him in the side. He slumped down against the wall, but the damage was done. Kaelyssa heard the sound of alarm horns below and was certain similar alarms were sounding at Fort Brunzig. She gritted her teeth. There was nothing to do but press on.

Dawnlord Vyros Nyarr paused during a brief lull in the battle to savor the warmth of the rising sun. So far they had been successful. The sloping hillside was littered with the corpses of Khadoran dead. The ambush could not have gone more smoothly, and Vyros' estimate on the range of Fort Brunzig's cannons had proven to be accurate. Those powerful guns had sounded only once, their shells falling well short of his position. The enemy clearly expected them to close on the fortress and was holding their fire for that eventuality.

> THE HUNTER FORCE SWEPT FORWARD AS IF OF ONE MIND, USING BLADES TO TAKE DOWN THE SOLDIERS AND DRIVERS QUICKLY

The second wave was advancing now. Lines of troops in heavier armor were marching down the slope toward their position while the looming edifice of Fort Brunzig watched from the heights of the next sloping hill. The Khadoran kommanders seemed determined not to underestimate the enemy again. The Khadorans did not know who they were or what they were capable of doing. Vyros had hoped this would make them somewhat slow to react, but thus far the Khadorans had shown no evidence of such apprehension, and their numbers were greater than in his grimmest projections.

Lines of Dawnguard stood ready, with invictors and their rifles to the fore, backed by sentinels and their heavy blades and joined by several groups of destors on the extremes of both flanks. A number of ghost snipers and Stormfall archers waited behind the Dawnguard to deliver their firepower, as did several teams of mage hunters. Myrmidons were scattered among them, unmoving but conveying readiness to those who stood near to them by the vibration of their steel frames and the deep hum of their fields and engines.

Several copses of woods along the hill and numerous clusters of boulders and other rocky formations afforded the Dawnguard some cover, but the heavy infantry headed in their direction looked formidable. Men-O-War formed the hard center, with several Khadoran warjacks to the rear, primarily Destroyers armed with long-ranged bombards. Long lines of Iron Fang pikemen in their plated armor and heavy shields advanced in disciplined formation alongside and behind the steam-powered vanguard. It was an altogether fearsome-looking force, the true might of the enemy, and Vyros was ready to meet it strength for strength. He relished the opportunity. The fact that they outnumbered him only increased his desire to defeat them on their own ground.

Vyros moved his myrmidons into position and marched behind the main line issuing commands to his subordinates. His Griffon myrmidons looked particularly eager to charge forward, crouched as they were with their halberds extended and shields set before them. He saw Ravyn with her forces at one of the more sheltered but steeper sections of the incline, and with a gesture she indicated they were ready. Mounted on his steed next to Ravyn was the fane knight Skeryth Issyen. The sight of the man irritated Vyros. The scion of House Issyen had avoided speaking to the dawnlord or any of his senior officers during the expedition, which Vyros considered a cowardly display of disrespect for a man of his birth and station. The breach in etiquette galled him, but he had decided to overlook it for the present. Ravyn could have her hound, so long as he proved useful in the battle.

The dawnlord felt a tingling awareness at the back of his head, an impression he at first attributed solely to Ravyn's proximity. The sensation grew stronger, and he looked up the slope toward the Khadoran warjacks, raising an eyebrow as he realized at least one human warcaster must be among them. Ravyn's face reflected a similar anticipation when he looked back to her. With a flick of his arm and a mental command Vyros sent his hawk Jyren to wing, telling her to find this enemy.

The battle raging inside the underground chambers of the bunker threatened to turn into utter chaos as teams broke off to deal with incoming threats. After cornering and eliminating a group of soldiers firing on her from a long, dark storage chamber, Kaelyssa doubled back, passing the bodies of several Greylords bleeding out onto the corridor floor. The mage hunters who had intercepted them had already moved on. Occasional bursts of rifle fire echoed through the halls, and the iron smell of spilled blood mixed with the char of blasting powder in the air. Kaelyssa moved through the complex with caution and predatory grace as she sought her target. The passageways were too small for her myrmidons, but she wished she had a Chimera at her back. Amid these tunnels and sharply angled corridors, ambush was a constant danger.

Kaelyssa tapped her arcane talents to project her senses through the walls around her. Her senses provided her with an undeniable edge even with the chaos of motion throughout the bunker. Despite the confusion, she could still call upon her magic to send runebolts through interior walls as if they were not there.

Above her she felt an explosion of ice magic and sensed its destructive power freezing several mage hunters to death. Momentarily distracted, she almost overlooked a group of Khadorans lying in ambush in a room just to her right. She felt a twinge of warning as she neared the open doorway and immediately rolled forward into a tumble as metal shot tore holes in the stone where she had passed. She heard footsteps behind her and saw her third team round the corner, trying to catch up with her. She held up a palm, and they skidded to a stop. Reaching her senses through the intervening wall she picked up three vague forms, likely two Winter Guard and a Greylord. This sense was only tangentially like sight, but it was as if she could perceive the individuals as vague patterns of light and motion. Those who could wield magic, like a Greylord, were marked by an inner illumination representing gathered power.

Kaelyssa fired three runebolts in quick sequence, each vanishing the instant they left her cannon to flicker past the intervening wall and sink into her targets one by one. The smoky after-image of their presence faded to her heightened perception along with their lives. Kaelyssa waved her team to follow once again as she turned to descend deeper into the complex.

The silence in which her people operated gave the violence in the bunker an eerie one-sided din limited to the shouts and gunfire of the Khadorans. Every minute that passed, Kaelyssa's concern for the success of the mission increased. She ruefully remembered her naive words to Ravyn during their last meeting. Nothing could ever be simple.

Just below she sensed a far stronger presence that shone brightly with power. It must be the warcaster, Aleksandra

IOSAN KNIFE

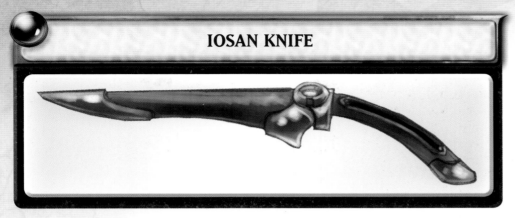

Zerkova. There was also a strangely heavy blankness, something large that even her senses could not penetrate. *Could this be Nyssor? Was he truly here?* She felt her pulse race at the possibility, but knew she must stay focused. That enigma would have to wait until she had eliminated Zerkova and secured the bunker. She wished she knew how things fared with Ravyn and the dawnlord, but she could not presume she had the luxury of time.

Acting in concert, Vyros' invictors fired their heavy rifles as a solid barrage into the advancing Khadoran lines, but the hefty armor held up to the punishment. The Stormfall archers rained down explosive arrows, while the ghost snipers delivered their deadly shots to key targets of opportunity. Still the enemy closed, unfazed by their losses. They had a clear and obvious numerical superiority and seemed intent on crushing the Iosans by sheer weight if need be.

Invictor rifles were stout pieces of gear, attached at top and bottom with massive chopping blades for when battle closed. It soon became clear they would be forced to deal with the Khadorans hand-to-hand. One line of invictors smoothly fell back while the next line fired, and the sentinels advanced to stand ready behind them. Energy blasts from Manticores and Phoenixes blazed into the enemy, killing a few more, but then the lines met and clashed. The Khadorans had the advantage of higher ground. At Vyros' command the sentinels surged forward to support the invictors as the battle was joined in full.

The dawnlord's tactics had served to preserve his strength along the line despite the brutal assault, accumulating an impressive tally of kills. Nonetheless, he loathed this sort of defensive engagement, where the initiative belonged to the enemy. He had to remind himself that his objective was purely to endure. They had already bought time for the strike teams at the bunker. That the Khadorans were present in far greater strength than expected added a major complication to their planned withdrawal. Their forces would be able to reach safety only if he broke this Khadoran attack.

The time had come for him to lend his own blade to the fray. "Scyir Lenfaren, with me!" Vyros commanded to one of his nearest subordinates as he advanced alongside his myrmidons toward the section of his line where the Dawnguard had been spread thin. The Men-O-War pressed down hard upon them, led by axe-wielding men with shields and backed by those laying to with massive double-handed hammers.

On Vyros' signal the scyir barked orders to his subordinate thanes, and squads of sentinels fell into line, marching quickly to keep pace with their lord. Above their heads the hawk Jyren gave a piercing cry. Vyros was as mentally connected to the bird of prey as to his myrmidons, and through her eyes he was able to look down from above and gain a perspective on the entire battlefield. He saw Khadoran warjacks moving rapidly toward their position. A thick-bodied Khadoran in warcaster armor and wearing a gas mask was impelling the 'jacks forward while loading a massive, multi-barreled firearm. An escort of soldiers with rifles, shields, and similar masks came with him, just behind the forward wall of Men-O-War.

Vyros sent a flow of power to two small, fleet Griffon myrmidons advancing toward the enemy at the left and right extremes of the dawnlord's control range. The one to the right crouched slightly with its shield and halberd readied and then leapt forward, its legs pumping with increasing momentum as it churned across the ground. Its power field flickered into visibility as it leapt over a stretch of rocks, momentarily negating the weight of its armored metal frame. To the left flank, the second Griffon performed a similarly enhanced rush, and both small myrmidons weaved adroitly through invictors and sentinels to crash into the steam-armored Khadorans precisely where Vyros needed them to be.

Dawnlord Vyros followed behind them, crying "Nyarr!" as he swept the massive blade of Justicar with both hands straight through the nearest Man-O-War. Driven by the momentum of his charge and augmented by his warcaster armor, the blade plunged through the man's shield and the armor below his left armpit and sliced upward to exit near his right shoulder, nearly cutting him in twain. Vyros did not pause to observe the resulting fountain of blood and gore but turned to drive the blade down into the helmet of the next Khadoran in line.

He was in the thick of it, with no room for thought but the sweep of his blade to parry and destroy. The nearest Griffon fought alongside him in perfect harmony, its moves corresponding with its master's. The Dawnguard sentinels clashed moments later after fanning out to engage the Iron Fangs with their massive blades. Meanwhile Vyros' heavy myrmidons made their way up a steeper incline toward the incoming Khadoran 'jacks. Incoming bombard fire began to hammer into them, almost depleting the power fields of the leading Phoenix and one of the Manticores. The Khadoran warcaster was close enough to bring his weapon to bear and dropped several invictors with deadly accurate shots while his Destroyers continued to fire explosive shells.

Vyros smiled. His gambit seemed to have worked, though at a cost. The Khadoran warcaster had moved close enough to be imperiled alongside his 'jacks, but this meant Vyros' own force was also at risk since a large formation of Iron Fangs rushed to intercept them. The Iron Fangs spread out as they advanced and encircled the sentinels to engage them pike-to-blade. Before they entirely closed the distance, dozens of grenades fired by soldiers behind them wearing gas masks launched over the heads of the front line. These grenades belched yellow smoke wherever they landed, and the Iosans were overcome by painful, choking fumes that invaded their lungs and burned their eyes.

Vyros cut a swath through the Iron Fangs, but it was clearly not enough to unnerve Fort Brunzig's veterans. Meanwhile, blasting pikes hammered into his Griffon. They obliterated its shield, crippled its legs, and speared it repeatedly like a downed boar. At Vyros' thought, Jyren plunged straight down and then turned sharply to streak in front of Ravyn—their prearranged signal to strike.

Ravyn and her forces emerged from the right flank and moved unerringly toward Vyros' position, carving through any Khadorans unfortunate enough to stand in their path. At their fore was a wing of Dawnlord Destors with Fane Knight Skeryth Issyen. This wedge of cavalry smashed into the Iron Fang Pikemen from an unexpected angle even as they tried to adjust their formation. The booming report of destor cannons resounded, and several pikemen dropped before their lances hit home.

Vyros's Phoenix was surrounded by pikemen, and he mentally commanded it to ignite with blue-white fire that poured forth to consume them. Similar fire ran along the length of its blade as it marched past the burning and screaming men to close on the nearest Destroyer. Its great fire-spewing sword hammered down repeatedly, set the enemy 'jack ablaze, and tore deeply into its heavily armored upper chassis. Under this punishing onslaught, the fire in the Destroyer's eyes was soon extinguished. One of Ravyn's Hydras launched a blaze of energy into a Juggernaut on the right side and then sprang forward to engage it, swinging its force-charged gauntlets against the Juggernaut's ice axe.

On the other side a Marauder lunged forward and took a single, fiery hit from the Phoenix's blade before it leveraged a pair of wedged ram-fists against the myrmidon's torso. There was a loud clang of metal as the piston rams sent the Phoenix tumbling downslope along the boulder-strewn hillside. It took with it several Dawnguard caught in its path. Impelled by Vyros' will, it quickly pulled itself back to its feet while Vyros directed the nearest Manticore to engage the new threat.

From the hawk's vantage he could see Ravyn was almost in position and the Khadoran heavy 'jacks had nearly been sufficiently distracted. Unfortunately the cagey enemy warcaster had kept a Juggernaut near him, and he was also shielded by a sizable contingent of the masked soldiers, who were maintaining rifle fire punctuated with choking gas grenades.

Vyros had to abandon the wider perspective afforded by his hawk's eyes to focus on his immediate surroundings. A number of hammer-wielding Men-O-War came to beset him. Each time one fell to his blade another arrived in its place. He was forced to preserve his arcane strength so he could keep his power field strong enough to deflect numerous blows. His plan had drawn the Khadoran warcaster forward, but now he was cut off from the nearest sentinels.

The dawnlord saw motion out of the corner of his eye and felt satisfaction at Ravyn's arrival. She drove straight toward the Khadoran warcaster with a surge of violent grace that was a wonder to behold. Hellebore was a blur in her hands as she swept into the warcaster's bodyguards like an apparition of death. Her assault sliced through breastplates, knocked aside shields, and severed weapons. Periodically she reversed the weapon to fire a round from the rifle barrel that also served as the halberd's shaft. Her bloody arrival unnerved the nearest Khadorans in a manner Vyros and his sentinels had failed to do.

Almost too late the Khadoran warcaster realized his peril. As the nearest soldiers collapsed under the weight of Ravyn's attack, mage hunters followed behind firing their crossbows. Additional myrmidons were closing on his position. Incoming fire deflected off his own power field, and he felt compelled to pull back, seeing he faced not one but two unknown warcasters. With a thrust of his hand the Khadoran warcaster sent a surge of violent arcane force toward the mage hunters while runes of power circled his arm.

The ground exploded just to Ravyn's left. Her power field shielded her from the worst of it, but several of her nearest subordinates were torn apart by flying rocks. The Juggernaut he had kept in reserve stepped forward to block a Gorgon's energy blast. As the enemy warcaster moved

19

back he ignited and hurled a red flare high into the air. Vyros could see that Ravyn was determined to reach the Khadoran, fighting through the intervening soldiers with almost desperate haste.

"Ravyn, wait!" Vyros called out in a booming cry, having apprehended the meaning of the flare. "Fall back to me!" It seemed a visible effort of will for Ravyn to give up her pursuit, but she reluctantly heeded his call.

The Khadorans began to pull back in something akin to a panic, leaving wounded behind as they scrambled up the slope. Sentinels and invictors harried their withdrawal until Vyros called his men to stand down. Ravyn came alongside him with a questioning look. He explained, "We are too far upslope." He pointed the fortress. "He hopes to bait us into range." Her eyes widened as she looked back to the squat edifice where Fort Brunzig seemed to scowl down upon them.

> WITH A SCREAMING OF INCOMING SHELLS THE AIR WAS SOON THICK WITH EXPLOSIONS AND CHOKING SMOKE.

Just at that moment the great fortress guns fired. With a screaming of incoming shells the air was soon thick with explosions and choking smoke. Vyros was close enough to be momentarily deafened, and for a moment the world reeled with punishing blasts. As the air began to clear and the ringing in his ears faded, he heard a spontaneous shout of relief from the Dawnguard as they realized they had cleared the range of the Khadoran guns. The entire hillside just yards from their forward position was shredded and pocked with craters.

Ravyn looked toward the retreating Khadoran force with a rueful expression at having come so close to eliminating one of the enemy's vital warcasters. She leaned heavily on Hellebore and wiped dirt, blood, and mud from her face with her other hand. "Do you think they will attack again?"

Vyros considered and shook his head. "No, not now. They will pull back to the fortress and await our next move. Likely they expect us to besiege Brunzig. We must disappoint them. I will withdraw my men slowly, so they do not fully realize what we intend. Go ahead to the bunker and check on your people."

Ravyn nodded and without another word left with her soldiers. The Dawnguard who watched them go observed the mage hunters with a measure of respect, a marked contrast to the barely restrained derision of only a few months ago.

Vyros passed orders to his subordinates, preparing for their departure. As much as he would have enjoyed a more decisive victory against the Khadorans, he knew that was not their purpose. He took some satisfaction in imagining how the Khadorans would react when the Iosans vanished. If Ravyn managed their withdrawal as planned, this sense of vulnerability should undermine the enemy's morale more than any number of casualties inflicted here today. They would never know the feeling of safety and security again.

Kaelyssa was locked on to the enemy at last, after finding her deep in the bowels of the facility, but the witch refused to stand her ground. Koldun Kommander Aleksandra Zerkova was in full flight, casting whatever subordinates she could find as chaff behind her with no apparent regard for their lives. The mage hunter warcaster was willing to oblige, periodically reloading her runebolt cannon. Kaelyssa's ability to fire through walls had shaken the enemy, but unfortunately the opportunity for a clean kill had yet to present itself.

She stepped past the twitching hand of another dead magziev and rounded a sharp turn of the deep corridor to walk straight into a blast of malignant and gripping cold. A spell of formidable power, it inflicted painful freezing burns across her skin as the joins in her warcaster armor momentarily locked with solid ice. Zerkova did not linger to strike again but kept moving.

With some difficulty, Kaelyssa shook her arm loose with a spray of frozen particles. She lifted her runebolt cannon and fired one of its glyph-inscribed projectiles. It pierced the warcaster's power field and plunged into the back of the woman's left thigh. Kaelyssa felt a surge of power as some of Zerkova's strength was mystically siphoned away through the runebolt. Zerkova grunted in pain but limped forward to smash open a heavy metal door at the terminus of the corridor. The cannon's reloading mechanism slotted another glyphed bolt in the firing groove as Kaelyssa fired again. The witch's survival instincts were finely honed, and she managed to duck into the next chamber and narrowly avoid the bolt, which skittered instead along the nearest wall in a spray of sparks.

The unnatural cold inhibiting Kaelyssa persisted for only a few seconds, and she continued the chase. On reaching the open door she was hit by a sudden gust of fast-moving air, thick with the smell of coal smoke. She could hear the chuffing sound of large steam engines. She dove and tumbled through the door, coming upright with her weapon at the ready. She saw she was in a large, natural cave, lit well enough by gas lanterns to reveal a Khadoran steam locomotive. It was already starting to lurch forward as its pistons cranked. Several Winter Guard fired in her direction from its middle car as she darted behind a stack of nearby crates for cover.

A Khadoran warjack at the top of a loading ramp stepped back after pushing a massive stone object into the open doors of the last car even as the train began to move forward. A trail of blood up the ramp suggested Zerkova had ducked inside. Kaelyssa was unable to sense the interior of that car, which indicated that its walled panels were warded. Leaning out from the crates to fire, she made quick work of the Winter Guard escorts.

That threat eliminated, Kaelyssa stepped out in time to see the Khadoran 'jack turn to face her. It was a battered, old, unarmed Juggernaut, likely modified for labor. It clenched its hands and stepped toward her even as the steam train began to pick up speed with a churning sound, pouring smoke into the vaulted ceiling of the chamber. Kaelyssa could sense Zerkova's will in the malevolent stare of the Juggernaut's glowing eyes. It lunged to seize her with unnatural alacrity, its massive, articulated metal hands guided by the other woman. Kaelyssa narrowly evaded it by leaping to the side.

Kaelyssa gestured and sent a surge of rending magic straight into the Khadoran 'jack. She heard the satisfying sound of metal shredding as its armor puckered and internal pistons and gears seized. She raced past the machine even as the short Khadoran train gained speed at an alarming rate, lightly burdened as it was by only three nearly empty cars.

Seeing a shadowed face peering out at her from the last car opening, Kaelyssa raised her cannon and fired, leveraging all her hate and frustration into the shot. She felt grim satisfaction as the runebolt hit, striking Zerkova in the shoulder and hurling her back into the darkness of the warded car. Unfortunately she could sense the warcaster cling stubbornly to life as the train shattered through the closed gate at the mouth of the cave tunnel and burst into the open.

The mage hunter teams watching that entrance added their own crossbow fire toward the moving cars, but they were firing blind. Gasping for breath but ignoring her burning lungs, Kaelyssa reached the cave opening at a full run. She felt certain Nyssor was on board that train. In one last, desperate attempt to stop it, she hurled a blast of arcane power ahead of the engine, but it was already too far away. The blast fell short and exploded the earth and wooden ties well behind the swiftly retreating train.

When Ravyn rejoined the mage hunters gathering to withdraw outside the bunker she listened to Kaelyssa's rushed summary of the failed mission in patient silence. The junior warcaster's voice trembled with anger and shame as she spoke and it was clearly an effort for her to control her emotions. She reported the facts as plainly as possible and without embellishment. "He was here, but now Nyssor is gone. I let him slip through my fingers. I take full responsibility."

"Enough." Ravyn stopped her, shaking her head. She did not reprimand her subordinate, as Kaelyssa was clearly expecting. "Sometimes circumstances are outside your control. We knew this would be difficult. You have confirmed Nyssor was here. This is a significant lead, and one we will follow." Ravyn looked up and saw the other mage hunters had started to gather closer. She waved them forward and spoke loudly enough for everyone to hear.

"We do not have much time, as the Khadoran reinforcements will arrive soon. We must withdraw. But I want you to know I am tremendously proud of what we have done here. This is but the first battle of a longer war, and that war will not be won in a single day. *We will find Nyssor.* Have faith! We quit this field today of our own choice, to regroup and prepare to strike again. Soon the enemy will know the full extent of our determination. Do not dwell on what could have been. Consider instead all we have done today." Her hand swept toward the open door of the bunker, where smoke poured from flames within and the bodies of their enemies littered the ground.

"We have marched unhindered deep into our enemy's lands. We have destroyed a base of their occultists, killing many who would harm Scyrah with unclean magic. We have proven that we can fight on ground of our choosing, that their borders mean nothing to us. Already they begin to fear us—as they should, for ours is a righteous cause. We will give them much more to fear in the days ahead."

Conviction shone in Ravyn's voice like sharpened steel, and as she spoke she watched the hunters' disappointment transform into resolve and belief. In time they would come to appreciate the scope of their accomplishment, but for now it was enough that they draw strength from the righteousness of their purpose.

Without another look at the carnage they had wrought, Ravyn led them from the hill to rejoin the marching Dawnguard. Already she had begun to think and plan, considering what next steps they should take to advance their purpose. Their forces were committed now, and the enemy blooded. From this day forward the battles would change, but the stakes remained the same: victory or extinction.

THE LONG FALL
HISTORY OF IOS

"Never on the face of Caen have so great a people fallen so far."

—*Ryvoas Vyre, Theologian and Historian of House Vyre*

We stand at a pivotal point in history with nothing less than the very survival of our people at stake. I am honored that the Retribution of Scyrah has asked me to author this summation of our history. I hope it will unite us in a shared understanding of our origins. We cannot look forward until we fully understand what has come to pass.

Our ancient days have become a mystery to us—ironic, given the copious records we know our ancestors maintained in the annals of the old empire. Those documents are forever lost to us, destroyed in the Cataclysm. The further we venture into the past, the more uncertain the ground we tread becomes. In areas where our lore is lacking I offer my best analysis, as a scholar who has devoted his life to the study of these matters.

THE GODS AND OUR ORIGINS

Throughout our existence, we have been closely bound to our gods. Whether guiding our people from across the Veld or walking among us in the flesh, the gods have shared in all our triumphs and tragedies through countless generations. By their guidance the Empire of Lyoss experienced an age of prosperity lasting almost six thousand years.

The genesis of the gods lies outside the scope of our understanding, as my research has discovered no document in their words describing their inception. The tales our priests relate of the gods arising from a union of the moons and the sun are likely allegorical, poetic flights of fancy. Yet whatever their origin, long before our creation eight gods dwelled in a palace called Lyoss and ruled a domain called the Veld.

Lacyr was the unquestioned ruler, the Narcissar of Ages. At her side was the Incissar of Hours, Ossyris. We know the gods waged war because Ossyris is named the Sovereign of Conflict and General of Lyoss. We do not comprehend the nature of their wars, but artists have depicted legions of ephemeral spirits marching at Ossyris' behest to patrol the Veld's borders. The gods described the Veld as an oasis surrounded by enemies. Any peace the gods enjoyed was earned through constant vigilance.

Beneath Lacyr and Ossyris were Ayisla and Nyrro. She was Nis-Arsyr of Night and Watcher of the Gates of Lyoss, and he was Arsyr of Day, Seneschal, and Lorekeeper. Last came the four gods of our seasons: Scyrah, Nis-Issyr of Spring and Healer of the Divine Court; Lurynsar, Issyr of Summer, Arms Master of Lyoss, and Chief of Scouts; Lyliss, Nis-Scyir of Autumn, Court Assassin, and Mistress of Poisons; and lastly Nyssor, the Scyir of Winter and Grand Crafter.

Whatever existence the gods led, it was Lurynsar who first observed mortal souls spilling into the distant wilds of the afterlife. On hearing of this discovery, Lacyr followed the path of these souls back to Caen and witnessed the barbarity of their existence. Despite the cruel and unclean habits of these creatures, the gods saw the potential buried within them. These human souls multiplied as their tribes spread, providing a bounty for their creator.

Lacyr was inspired to create her own people, but one more refined. She envisioned a deliberately sculpted species fit to inherit and subjugate the world. Lacyr became Potentate of the Living by giving life to our people while the goddess Scyrah served as midwife to soothe her birth pains. The Divine Court watched from beyond the mortal divide and guided us from the first days, teaching us law, civilization, agriculture, writing, and construction as well as the subtle arts of magic and the necessary arts of war.

To us the gods brought the coherent concepts of the present and the past, the ordered passage of the hours, and the division of the seasons as Caen followed its path around the sun. It was they who demonstrated how the cycles of the moons influenced wind, rain, and tide. The gods also embodied the natural process of life and death. Life begins in spring with Scyrah, governor of birth and growth, before passing into Issyr's summer heat. Life wanes in autumn with Lyliss before the quiet cold of winter shrouds Nyssor holding court, preparing the land for rebirth in spring.

Nyrro watched the day, and the sun represents our living years, while his counterpart Ayisla supervised night and the passage into death in her role as Suzerain of the Fallen. Our souls were borrowed from the gods, who regulated their cycle in the afterlife. When a soul passed on, it traveled to the afterlife and met Ayisla at the gates of the Veld to be appraised. Those judged worthy she allowed to pass into the domain of the gods, there to experience an eternity of grace. Others, judged unready, she sent back to be reborn. It is a sacred process now lost, perhaps beyond recovery.

SYMBOLS OF IOSAN GODS

Lacyr

Ossyris

Ayisla

Nyrro

Scyrah

Lurynsar

Lyliss

Nyssor

The gods bestowed upon us tremendous gifts. Blessed by the insight of the divine, our people advanced rapidly in natural science and other fundamental fields of knowledge. Mathematics, engineering, architecture, and arcane formulae came to us easily and swiftly. The seasonal cycle renewed our bodies even as they renewed the land, bestowing a life span longer than any other creature walking Caen. Time was our ally.

THE GOLDEN ERA AND THE EMPIRE OF LYOSS

The early years of our people were not all bliss and prosperity. There were numerous bloody wars between competing fiefdoms of our ancestors. They disagreed, and disagreements begat violence. In time, at the urging of the gods, a single voice of unity began to gather our people into what would become the Empire of Lyoss. The empire took the name of the palace of the gods as a sign of their approval and continued involvement.

Our ancestors honed the arts of war during the struggle for unification, and these skills served us well against external threats thereafter. They beat back human and skorne savages lurking at the fringes of the empire's borders. Eventually our ancestors made contact with the dwarves of Rhul, the only dim light of civilization outside Lyoss, albeit sequestered in a remote mountainous region far to the west. Lyoss saw them neither as a threat nor as competition.

Had events gone otherwise, in time the dominion of Lyoss would have stretched from the great waters of the east to those of the west. Eventually our reach would have extended even past the shores of Immoren to embrace continents beyond. The Orgoth would have stood no chance against our great empire.

Our golden era was long, but sadly we know little about it. Thousands of years of history are gone like a half-remembered dream. The continent was different in that age, with fertile plains and flowing rivers where today there is nothing but desert and desolation. Our capital, Nyshyl, sat at the heart of what is now a great rift dividing the continent. Nyrro's sun never shines on the ruins of Nyshyl, which were shattered to dust and are now cloaked in storm and punished by ceaseless lightning.

I have journeyed across the desert sands to the east to see the ruins of Osslarys, the closest of the known Lyossan ruins. At the height of the empire, Osslarys was nothing but a small and inconsequential outpost noted only for the productivity of its mines. Yet upon seeing the broken buildings I was overwhelmed with the majesty and splendor of what our ancestors had wrought. I can only imagine the wonders of ancient Nyshyl, a city stretching across the glorious River Hyless and boasting over two million souls. Every man and woman currently in Ios could have dwelled comfortably in Nyshyl with room for twice that number again.

We know precious few details of ancient Lyoss. Its rulership was shared by the collective eight great fanes of the gods. The central fanes in the capital administered the empire, while subordinate fanes supervised outlying regions. Lyoss was no utopia. Certainly it had its teeming poor, but the empire's wealth and agriculture were ample to feed all. Periodic upheaval and strife was put down by heavy-handed applications of force, and peace would once again dominate for a time.

In their wisdom the gods allowed our people considerable oversight of the organization and direction of daily life, but the fundamental guiding precepts came from their higher authority. It was only natural that our gods take part in governing our empire with their priests serving as their proxies or instruments as needed.

The only lingering dissatisfaction the people felt was an awareness of separation from our divine patrons. Five thousand years ago the eldest priests met at the Council of Anifaryl and resolved to address this distance. Why could we not share our lives as well as our afterlives with our gods? When they drew up plans for the Bridge of Worlds, Lacyr herself blessed its inception with approving omens.

THE BRIDGE OF WORLDS

No Iosan today can speak of the Bridge of Worlds without anger and regret, yet the bridge represented hope incarnate for our ancestors. The tireless efforts of millions labored four *hecyion* to transform a potentially impossible idea into reality. So great a project had never been attempted in the history of Caen and likely never will be again. Mortal and divine minds joined to create a tangible conduit from the world of the gods to the earth where mortals toiled.

The Bridge of Worlds was not metaphorical. It was a massive physical structure soaring into the sky above the capital. The architectural and mystical techniques developed during its creation became cornerstones of the engineering we still utilize today and were employed in the construction of our cities and great fane structures.

The most likely portrayal of the Bridge of Worlds depicts a soaring stone arch reaching into the sky to terminate at its apex as if it were one half of a bridge intended to cross a mountain ravine. The missing half existed as spirit in the Veld, built by the gods and designed for perfect mystical alignment with its material counterpart. A linked series of hundreds of massive arcane generators were built into the cyclopean foundation, and a lattice of metal sigils was inlaid across the streets of the capital, extending for miles into the surrounding lands.

The Bridge of Worlds was intended to be a permanent road the gods could traverse at will. A vast variety of blessings and advancements were expected to result from the close proximity of the gods and the more immediate access to their counsel and wisdom. The bridge's construction occupied two hundred and fifty years and levied a cost in lives and materials we could never again afford. It should have persisted as the greatest wonder of the world.

Something went terribly wrong the moment the bridge was put to use. The hour of glory upon them, our ancestors activated the Bridge of Worlds and watched as the gods stepped from the Veld. In gatherings across Lyoss millions of our people congregated to celebrate the arrival of the divine. This did in fact begin a new age, but one born in unimaginable catastrophe and devastation rather than golden glory. We call this event the Cataclysm.

THE CATACLYSM

As the gods stepped onto Caen, the Bridge of Worlds exploded in a torrent of wild arcane power. Only the repercussions hint at the scope of the event, and they were of the utmost extremity. Survivors even hundreds of miles away wrote of great pieces of flaming stone raining destruction upon them. Closer to the blast, waves of raw force crushed everything into fine dust. A searing wall of heat instantly consumed everyone near the explosion—perhaps a blessing in some respects.

The explosive force was so great Immoren itself was sundered. Along what was once the vibrant River Hyless opened The Abyss, a chasm so deep it reaches the hot arteries of the world where molten stone flows like blood. Nyshyl, our great and glorious capital, was obliterated. Where it stood, nothing remains except a gaping hole in the world.

Survivor records describe unnatural blue-white fires in the wake of this explosion that burned indefinitely without fuel and could not be extinguished. The very stones

IOSAN CALENDAR AND DATES

The Iosan calendar is a complex timekeeping system rooted in astronomical observations. Arcane and religious scholars apply mystical significance to its cycles. The "long calendar," or *hecyion*, details the passage of time in 64-year increments. Most Iosan citizens prefer the *cyion* or "short calendar," based on an 8-year cycle. A hecyion comprises eight cyion.

Iosans emphasize seasons rather than months as the primary yearly division. Months remain a significant time interval by which the seasons are divided, of a length equal to the cycle of Caen's largest moon. Iosans do not divide months into weeks but refer to "half-months" and "quarter-months." Iosan astronomers utilize more esoteric terms for longer celestial cycles.

The numbering of years in Ios is based on a division separating the time before and after the Cataclysm. The ^ symbol designates the Cataclysm and is placed before or after the date to show the relationship between the two. For example, the Empire of Lyoss was unified 6,147 years before the Cataclysm, in the year 6147^. To reconcile this numbering system with human date numbering it must be considered that the Cataclysm was 3,966 years before the zero date on the human calendar which represents the initial declaration of rebellion against the Orgoth. If the current year by human reckoning is 608 AR, the Iosan equivalent is ^4574.

Some scholars prefer using cyion or hecyion rather than decades or centuries. The date ^4574 can be written as 71*hy*3*cy*6 in this nomenclature (71 hecyions + 3 cyions + 6 years = 4574).

burned like cordwood. Weather patterns across Immoren changed irrevocably, and what was once a small desert far to the southwest of Nyshyl would become a vast and nearly impassible waste. Along the Abyss, freakish energies combined with seismic upheaval to birth the Stormlands, a region of lightning and unrelenting rain and wind that persists even today.

Only one word can describe the impact of this terrible event on Lyoss: annihilation. Our empire and most of our people were simply gone. Tens of millions died instantly, and millions more perished in the aftermath of unnatural weather and spreading fires. Those inhabiting the fringes starved or were set upon by predators. Were it not for our gods, I am convinced our people would have been no more.

Fortunately our creators were unwilling to relinquish what they had shaped. The gods had survived the explosion and stood among the people, where they could expend their divine strength to shelter as many as possible from the devastation. Over the next decade, the gods marched the survivors west away from the horrors consuming the east.

During their passage the people were beset by countless terrors and were too many for the gods to protect fully. At a crucial juncture in the journey, a host of brave warriors made the decision to sacrifice their own lives to preserve the safety of thousands of others. These were the Dawnguard, an ancient order then devoted to Nyrro. The Dawnguard moved to the rear of the long procession of evacuees to battle the relentless aggressors. Most of these courageous knights, the surviving remnants from the ancient House Nyarr, died amid the sands of the expanding desert so that the people could escape. Indeed, some believe all who bore the name Nyarr perished in the crossing, but nobles of that house insist the bloodline survived.

THE FOUNDING OF IOS

Our people settled into the lands of Ios on the advice of the gods, who saw in this place the potential for us to recover and thrive. The Mistbough and Archenbough Forests were lush and vibrant, with fertile farmland to the north and the entire region sheltered between towering walls of imposing mountains.

Tentative contact was renewed with Rhul, as that long-standing nation had always been cordial to Lyoss. Our ancestors told Rhul no more than was necessary but opened a channel for future communication and trade.

It is no coincidence that Aeryth Dawnguard and the Gate of Storms were the first structures built in Ios. The former served both as a fortress watching to the east and as a monument to the Dawnguard lost in the crossing. Many liegemen from houses torn apart in the Cataclysm joined

the Dawnguard and swore themselves oath-brothers as they offered their bodies to stand for those who had fallen. Our ancestors feared fresh horrors might follow them across the wastes, so Aeryth Dawnguard stood vigil. The Gate of Storms soon stood ready in the case Rhul decided to test our resolve.

Next came the Gate of Mists. Over time, the size and the scope of this great fortress have increased greatly from their humble origins. In the early centuries humanity was not a concern to us, being a motley collection of barbaric tribes. It would be thousands of years before we would look at humanity again with fresh eyes.

At last the survivors of the Cataclysm had a place to rest and heal, both as individuals and as a people. The loss of Lyoss was horrible, and yet the gods walked among us. The comforting presence of the Divine Court inspired our people to tremendous efforts. They dreamed that in time Ios would stand even mightier than Lyoss had. With the gods present, anything was possible.

CITY OF IRYSS

A long period of construction followed the initial settlement. Every surviving citizen contributed. Our ancestors worked quarries and mines and then laid the foundation of new cities, roads, fortifications, farms, and all such necessary elements of civilization. The old arts were put to use as much as possible, but much knowledge had already been lost. Sadly, we will never know the scope of that gap.

The eight original cities of Ios were each dedicated to one member of the Divine Court, and at the heart of each city they constructed a great temple to serve as that god's dwelling place. These fanes were true homes of the gods, not mere houses of worship. Our ancestors knew they must create halls and chambers fit for the divine. They were aware that even their best efforts would be crude and barren in comparison to the sublime palace in the Veld crafted by Nyssor's hands.

Given this, it is no wonder that such tremendous construction projects were undertaken even in these desperate early years. Monuments of towering stone they erected and blessed with sacred runes. The gods had crossed the Bridge of Worlds to be with us, and the fanes were one small way of offering thanks for their protection.

It is beyond tragic that most of those original cities no longer stand. We have not been adequate stewards of the gifts left us by our forebears. Our capital is the only great city we have retained in pristine condition. Shyrr is a city promised eternally to the devotion of Narcissar Lacyr, creator of our people. This city became the center of our civilization, and here our ancestors created the most magnificent fane. It was raised above a maze of tunnels and chambers that would later serve as the center of Iosan government and provide a meeting place for all the priesthoods and the gods themselves.

Iryss is our second largest surviving city, and it shows far greater signs of the toll of unkind years. Those dwelling there have done what they can to maintain it, as this was the former home of Scyrah, then the Nis-Issyr of Spring. Her fane is kept as if the goddess were in residence, even though she chose eventually to inhabit Shyrr. The last remaining of the old cities is Lynshynal, created as the home of Lurynsar, Issyr of Summer and Lord of the East Forest. Sheltered under the branches of the Archenbough, in recent years the city has become increasingly industrial and is now dominated by forges and workshops. Lynshynal remains untouched by the harsh bite of winter, some insist as a blessing of its former master, but it is certainly not the beauteous city it once was.

The five cities now lost to us I will recount briefly. Of these, Issyrah to the west is the most recently ruined, fallen to the rapacious appetite of a dragon just two hundred years ago. It was created in devotion to Ayisla, the Nis-Arsyr of Night. Once its boulevards were lit as bright as day at midnight to accommodate the nocturnal habits of its populace. In the east was Shaeross, the home of Ossyris. As befits the Incissar of Hours and General of Lyoss, this fane was second in grandeur only to Shyrr. The gleaming Eversael was the city devoted to Nyrro, Arsyr of Day. This was our first completed and northernmost city, located just to the southeast of Aeryth Dawnguard. I will speak further of this place anon. South of the Gate of Storms was Shaelvas, also called the City of Wind, devoted to Lyliss, Nis-Scyir of Autumn. Lastly, the almost mythical city of Darsael. Its existence was nearly expunged from the written record over a thousand years ago, but this small city was once devoted to Nyssor, Scyir of Winter. Perhaps we will soon have the power to begin its restoration.

Considerable esteem was attached to the major surviving noble houses of the old empire. The leaders of these houses took initiative in the rebuilding of our culture and earned their places in the new Consulate Court that arose as the governing body. These became the 15 *hallytyr*, or "high houses," standing above an echelon of hundreds of lesser noble houses.

We look back on those days in envy but it is worth remembering that even then the gods did not often walk among the people. They preferred to isolate themselves inside their fanes to focus on higher matters. Each of the gods periodically emerged to grace the people or to travel to Shyrr to speak in private council with Lacyr. They joined seasonal celebrations and gatherings but otherwise maintained their privacy. While no one was willing to intrude upon the gods to question them, many wondered whether they yearned for the Veld even as they watched over Ios.

THE GREAT MALAISE

It was centuries before our people could perceive that an inexplicable ill had taken root. The first sign came with the onset of old age and the consumptive impact of diseases afflicting our elders. Given the tremendous longevity and health we had previously enjoyed as a people, this was a terrifying development.

Today we take for granted the withering of our final years, often just three hundred years after birth. For this first generation in Ios such rapid aging was unprecedented. Death from violence was familiar, but being consumed from within was not. Several persistent epidemics tore through Ios within the first millennium after the Cataclysm. For the first time our gods had no ready answers, although Scyrah and Lacyr miraculously cured as many of the afflicted as they could and Lyliss mercifully eased the final suffering of countless others.

It would be some time before our forebears recognized other aspects of this decline, such as a tremendous reduction in births. Given the spaced occurrence and private nature of such matters, each family suffered in silence, making it difficult to gauge the scope of the decline. Eventually scholars concluded that despite apparent prosperity, population numbers were in alarming recession.

Our ancestors begged the gods for a solution but received no answer. Resentment of the gods grew, with inhabitants of each city blaming the patron of another. Some found it suspicious that Scyrah had no solution, as her domain had always included fertility and birth. But by far the most popular targets were Lyliss and Nyssor, the gods of autumn and winter, given the qualities of those seasons in the cycle of life. These accusations led even to occasional bloodshed between citizens of the different cities, each protective of their patron god. The strong stigma associated with Darsael in particular has its roots in this era, eventually prompting a division of our people we have only recently learned to regret.

The gods attempted intervention, and for a time births surged and the people rejoiced in an era of prosperity. This hope was to prove short-lived. Ios entered a recurring cycle of false hopes and disillusionment that would last three thousand years. Twice more, after centuries of decline the gods tried to correct the problem with public demonstrations of divine power. Each time this provided only a brief respite before the problem returned worse than before.

Our people entered a widespread malaise and spent this era avoiding the facts before their eyes. Some say our citizens suffer from this same malady today. Our ancestors turned inward, isolated themselves, and sought distraction by idle entertainments and frivolous diversion. The inheritors of the survivors of Lyoss lost their sense of unity. The cities became disconnected, and roads succumbed to decay. The priesthoods no longer communicated between the fanes as they once had, instead focusing solely on the needs of their resident gods. Secrets and suspicion propagated and led to bursts of violent feuds between noble houses. The Consulate Court became powerless as a reflection of our people.

EXODUS OF THE GODS

I believe our gods early suspected that saving our people would require them to leave us. They studied the issue for many years trying to shape reality by divine providence in order to remain. At last in the year ^3126 they made an announcement to the entire populace: they would leave our world. This event at last united our isolated cities in a shared sense of alarm.

The gods revealed they too were suffering and their strength waned. The longer they were away from the Veld, the weaker their powers became. Their arrival had begun a cosmological imbalance that made it increasingly difficult for them to perform their divine functions. Our vitality is inextricably linked to the strength of our gods. The only solution was for the gods to reclaim the Veld and resume oversight of their domains. Unfortunately, any attempts to return met a seemingly impenetrable barrier between the spiritual and material worlds.

They did not explain where they hoped to find a place of egress, only that we would never see them again. Their eventual success would restore the proper balance of life and death. After this proclamation, the gods gathered at the great fane to Ossyris to conduct their final ceremonies. As the place in Ios where the gods had last convened, this fane thereafter was considered sacred and entry forbidden. The high priest of Ossyris invoked a powerful bane there, stating that none would walk its halls until their god returned. To our knowledge this bane has never been violated.

Despite whatever sorrows our ancestors felt at the departure of the gods, their exodus nonetheless brought hope. The gods had taken action and embarked upon a pilgrimage for our mutual salvation. For decades faith and industry rallied across Ios as citizens endeavored to make ready for our renewal.

It was at this time that Nyssor's people, those living in Darsael, abandoned their homes and began a lengthy migration out of Ios. The historians of the time preferred to let this event pass almost unremarked, and in later centuries there was a systematic effort to erase mention of Darsael to the degree that its existence has almost been forgotten. What few records we have indicate the populace was shepherded by a prophet named Aeric. Shortly after the departure of the gods, he claimed to have received a vision from Nyssor instructing him to lead his people away.

The people of Darsael were few in number and had long been shunned by the other Iosan communities, as devotion to Nyssor was unpopular. This god symbolized the end of life. The departure of his people may even have been welcomed as the first sign of better times to come. Our ancestors were desperate for "winter's end." We know now that the people of Darsael would become the Nyss, but Ios had little contact with these cousins for a thousand years.

Darsael was the first city to be abandoned, but in intervening centuries many more followed. The priests of each fane continued their holy duties, but the outlying cities withered as inhabitants gave up family homes and moved inward. Shaelvas was the next to be cast off and reclaimed by the wilds, and even the once-glorious Eversael became little more than the ceremonial grounds used to induct recruits into the ranks of the Dawnguard.

THE CULT OF NYRRO

Three hundred years after the exodus of the gods, the Fane of Nyrro in Eversael made an announcement that animated people across Ios. Nyrro had returned, they claimed, and brought with him glad tidings! Eversael became the center of joyous pilgrimages and offerings as citizens from every corner of Ios travelled there hoping to catch a glimpse of the god and hear his word. Tremendous festivals and feasts were held in the streets as the city experienced a rebirth. The priesthood encouraged these festivals with fresh revelations, much to the unease of the other fanes.

For years this new cult to Nyrro multiplied, but not all fell under its spell. Those wise enough to be skeptical contended it was peculiar that the priests continued to prevaricate in revealing the god's full message, and stories of his sightings grew increasingly fantastic. Dark rumors began to circulate outside of Eversael: the priesthood was said to be involved in unseemly rites within hidden chambers beneath their fane. Some who traveled to Eversael were never heard from again.

Then a survivor who had escaped the dungeons of the city fled to Aeryth Dawnguard and affirmed that the clergy had murdered any who sought to reveal their secrets. His story was corroborated when he led Dawnlord Chrylos Nyarr to a mass grave site.

We still do not entirely understand what led to the corruption of these once-holy men. Perhaps it was nothing more than an attempt to regain influence lost after Eversael was abandoned. It is possible the instigators initially believed they were acting in the interests of the people by restoring hope. Clearly these priests fell to the darker whispers of their souls.

The Dawnguard were infuriated at this betrayal. Nyrro had long been their patron god, and their affiliation with the priesthood had been close for millennia. In their eyes, these acts disgraced their order and therefore justice fell to them. The entire Dawnguard assembled to march from its fortress and descend on Eversael. Bound, dragged from their fane, and shamed into confession in view of their shocked followers, these priests admitted to a long litany of blasphemies. Dawnlord Chrylos Nyarr executed the leaders with his own blade and left his soldiers to deal with the rest. The cult evaporated and its survivors fled, leaving Eversael abandoned once more.

Eversael has since been avoided. Rumors persist that the unhallowed fane is haunted and cursed; there is even evidence to suggest that some members of the priesthood avoided execution and transformed themselves into eldritch, unholy creatures that feed on life to evade death. After this incident the Dawnguard divorced itself from any

CORRUPT PRIESTS OF NYRRO EVADED MORTALITY BY BECOMING ELDRITCH.

connection to Nyrro. A strong undercurrent of respect for the god lingers among pious members of the order, but they prefer to keep these sentiments private.

The brutal lesson inflicted on this corrupted fane served as a warning to forestall other attempts to exploit the absence of the gods. The influence of the remaining six fanes was reduced, and the spiritual belief of Ios never recovered. Soon this faith was to receive an even more grievous injury.

THE RIVENING

Fears that something terrible might have happened to the Divine Court were confirmed seven hundred years after the exodus of the gods. Across Ios, priests suddenly fled the great fanes screaming and ranting. Thus began the Rivening, a calamity with as profound an impact on our people as the Cataclysm.

The most detailed, if confused, accounts of this period are from witnesses at the heart of Shyrr. It was as if a wave of insanity consumed the minds of every priest. One high priest walked into the Consulate Court and calmly slit the throat of the House Syllrynal consul before being subdued. Several priests steeped themselves in oil, lit themselves on fire, and ran screaming down the streets. Others fell into murderous frenzies, stalking the streets for victims even as they wept and prayed. Most survivors were convinced they were witnessing the final end of civilization.

Had this madness been isolated to Shyrr it would have been terrible enough, but similar incidents occurred throughout Ios. Issyrah is said to have suffered even worse than the capital, as several of its priests tore out their own eyes in the open market and prompted frantic riots and subsequent acts of arson and looting. A large portion of western Issyrah was consumed in flames and had to be rebuilt. From this point forward the Fane of Ayisla in the city was shunned as a cursed place.

Iryss suffered the least although even this city was not unscathed. The priests of the Fane of Scyrah suffered a considerably milder variation of the dementia overtaking their brethren in other fanes. Many wandered the streets dazedly spouting gibberish, but they were less inclined to violence. These priests recollected their wits relatively swiftly, suffering only a few hours of raving confusion, whereas many priests of the other fanes never recovered.

The most chilling example of the madness beset Shaeross, the city of Ossyris. Having heard no word from the city in the weeks following the riots, Shyrr dispatched messengers to offer aid. These emissaries found the city gates sealed and no guards in attendance. When they forced their way inside they were confronted with the horror of streets piled with citizens murdered and soldiers fallen on their own blades.

No one has been able to reconstruct precisely what transpired in Shaeross. Ossyris' priests had long ago left their god's fane, which had become known as the Forbidden Temple. For centuries they had maintained residence at the city's central garrison where they assumed leadership. Such service to both the military and the god had long been an accepted tradition for the priests of the Sovereign of Conflict. Some have suggested that the Rivening madness was contagious in Shaeross. One small comfort was that the death toll might have been far higher had thousands of citizens not left before the massacre. Still, the city became another proof of the slow doom of our people, and it was never again inhabited.

Some stricken priests recovered from their madness thanks to the ministrations of Scyrah's clergy. Asked what had happened, they haltingly described an abrupt and severe mental shock followed by a complete sense of isolation from the gods. Subsequently all Iosan priests except those belonging to the Fane of Scyrah found they could no longer channel the divine through prayer. It was this that gave rise to the term "Rivening" to describe the violent severance of the connection between the gods and their clergies. Afterward many deduced that perhaps most of the gods were lost, even destroyed. Those priests sane enough to reach this conclusion fell into despair, and many took their own lives.

Such news was impossible to silence, although some attempts were made to keep the scope of the Rivening a secret. Word spread more quickly than expected and prompted panic and chaos. The Consulate Court was largely powerless to bring order. They summoned soldiers from the interior garrisons to quell several riots, but that only exacerbated the situation and resulted in additional loss of life. In the weeks and months following the initial uproar it was Scyrah's priests who eventually calmed the people. Their presence provided at least some small spark of spiritual reassurance, for their powers had not been sundered.

One of the most profoundly disturbing manifestations of the Rivening was the onset of Iosan infants born without souls. Before this time there is no record of complications of this nature. Every expectant parent in Ios has come to dread this possibility. The soulless are born with black, empty eyes. They never cry at birth and only stare blankly up at their horrified mothers.

Soulless births were thankfully infrequent at first, but they have slowly increased with each passing hecyion. The most likely cause of this phenomenon is the vanishing of the goddess Ayisla. As the Watcher of the Gates and Suzerain of the Fallen, this goddess was responsible for the natural processes of reincarnation and passage into the afterlife. With her gone, it may be that souls slated for reincarnation are incapable of returning from the Veld to Caen. If this is the case, soulless represent empty vessels forever awaiting the arrival of missing pieces of themselves.

Without the bulwark of the Fane of Scyrah, Ios might have collapsed into anarchy and self-destruction during the dark decades to come. Even with their aid this was a time of grief and sorrow as the people came to grips with the likelihood that most of the gods had been destroyed. We had shattered our empire and borne the deaths of untold millions to bring the gods to Caen, and now they were gone.

Collectively the Divine Court began to be referred to as the Vanished. The fanes continued to honor all gods in their seasonal ceremonies, but for many citizens such efforts only reinforced their sense of loss. Ios began to shift from the worship of eight gods to focus on the one they dared hope had endured.

ONSET OF THE SOULLESS

The soulless are distinctly different from other Iosans. In addition to their black eyes, the soulless evidence few emotional responses. Their minds are as keen as other Iosans', but they interpret instructions literally and have little sense of ambition, self, or motivation. They lack empathy and demonstrate no sign of conscience, even when instructed in the concept of morality.

Most citizens, and particularly the Fane of Scyrah, deem such children anathema. It is considered a necessary mercy to kill them at birth. This policy arose after several isolated instances where adult soulless committed atrocities with no apparent remorse or awareness that they had done wrong. There is no sign that these inclinations are common, but the Fane of Scyrah decreed such beings were unnatural and must not be allowed to live.

Those who have spent time with soulless insist they are not completely devoid of emotions but rather experience a muted echo of natural feelings. They appear capable of becoming attached to certain individuals from whom they more readily accept instruction. It is common for parents of such offspring to try to preserve their lives. Similarly, midwives within the Fane of Scyrah often balk at killing the infants. Over time a conspiracy has arisen within the profession whereby many practitioners defy fane law by rescuing soulless children to deliver them to the Retribution of Scyrah, where they will at least be given shelter and be raised to fulfill a purpose.

SCYRAH RETURNS

It was almost a century after the Rivening that fragile hope was reaffirmed. Late one evening in the winter of ^3932, witnesses atop the outer walls of Shyrr saw an approaching figure. A hauntingly beautiful woman entered into the city after pushing open the great sealed gates with no more effort than turning aside a cloth curtain. Without speaking a word, she walked the central avenue toward the city's heart, gathering a steadily increasing throng of astonished onlookers as word spread that perhaps the divine Scyrah had returned. With dazed memories, all who described this scene after the fact noted its dreamlike quality overwhelming their senses.

This fog added to confusion over her initial identification; the goddess of spring had always been depicted as an eternally youthful, vibrant maiden, but the woman they saw before them seemed older and weary. She was still beautiful, but her expression suggested sorrow and loss. The complexity of emotion and meaning in her reappearance gave us one of our most frequently depicted scenes in art. Her presence was a welcome relief, and yet her silence provoked more concern than joy. She offered no glad tidings, no reassurances. The gods had departed saying they would never return; their passage to the Veld was the only hope of our people. What could Scyrah's return mean except proof of failure or defeat?

Scyrah's priesthood awaited her at the central fane in Shyrr, originally devoted to Narcissar Lacyr. The goddess walked into their midst and was not seen outside again. The rest of Shyrr was left standing in the streets in baffled amazement.

It would be long centuries before the Fane of Scyrah admitted she had not spoken to them upon her return. The clergy remained tight-lipped about her condition, offering empty reassurances and asking for prayer and patience in equal measure. The fane's standing as the one surviving priesthood in Ios was reaffirmed by the widely witnessed arrival of the goddess. This served for a time to preserve the faith of the people, however thin. Yet its ongoing silence on vital questions divided the clergy from the people. In the period immediately after the Rivening, the Fane of Scyrah had helped heal the community, but at this time they turned inward with no energy to spare for anything beyond attending to the goddess.

As a sympathetic and pious historian I can grant these priests some forbearance. Doubtless they feared shattering what small hope had been restored by the goddess' return. What we know now that the citizens of the time did not was that Scyrah collapsed soon after entering the Fane of Lacyr. She has been in a state akin to slumber ever since, though her mind is active and the priests feel her connection to them. The Auricant Velahn insists Scyrah imparts wisdom and instructions by subtle portents and the occasional whispered word. All her will and little strength are focused on maintaining our people.

Most frightening of all about Scyrah's malady was its ability to afflict a divine being embodying living vitality itself. Many have theorized it was this wellspring that preserved her while the other gods succumbed. Others suggest Lacyr sacrificed herself to save Scyrah, knowing only the goddess of spring could hope to preserve Ios. Scyrah has provided no discernable clues as to what actually happened to her or the other gods.

My sympathies for the initial dilemma of Scyrah's priesthood are undone by the inexcusable act of concealing the extent of her malady for centuries. Those are years upon years lost to us forever. It was not until ^4296 that the fane announced Scyrah was not recovering as many had hoped but was actually dying, her once-fervid vitality draining away. They predicted she would perish in less than six hecyion. As I write this, we now stand at fewer than eighty years from this prophesied doom. The last fragile leaves of our people barely cling to the branch.

ROOTS OF THE RETRIBUTION

Shortly after the Rivening a number of theologians and occult scholars began a systematic examination of the cosmological dilemma. This was a bold endeavor given the scope of the issue, the turmoil of the period, and the tendency of most citizens toward despair. I am proud to say a number of my own ancestors, Adeptis Hylesh Vyre among them, were instrumental in these pioneering studies. These were the first systematic attempts to document and understand the exact manner in which the loss of the gods had affected the people of Ios, both during life and after death.

Safe within the confines of our borders, until this time Ios had been largely ignoring the outside world. Nevertheless a few emissaries and ambassadors had been sent abroad as a measure to protect our people from unexpected threats. Such tasks were risky even in the best of times, as humanity was fractured into a thousand crude city-states, each with its own customs, but our emissaries had learned enough to communicate with such people. That changed when a hostile human power called the Orgoth landed on the shores of Immoren to begin a long campaign of conquest. Our ambassadors were killed on any contact with this invading empire. The Orgoth eventually attempted to invade Rhul's southern border and inflicted severe casualties before being driven back. Our forces were kept at the ready should they attempt the same violence against us.

SCYRAH IN THE INNER FANE BELOW SHYRR

The Consulate Court realized they must implement more covert means to keep apprised of events beyond our borders. They initiated an effort to observe these foreign powers in hopes of better understanding humanity in general and the Orgoth in particular. This was the first time an external power seemed capable of posing a significant threat to our people.

Among the most surprising information gathered by these efforts was the sudden proliferation of arcane lore among humanity, distributed in a strangely systematic pattern. Before this time it was generally believed humans lacked any insight into this art. The Orgoth had been rumored to invoke dire sorceries, which our scholars presumed to be the gifts of their loathsome gods. What puzzled agents abroad was evidence that an increasingly organized resistance against the Orgoth was utilizing arcane power that did not appear to be derived from either their erstwhile conquerors or their own gods.

This budding arcane lore proved instrumental in casting aside Orgoth dominion, albeit requiring long years of conflict. The pace at which these formerly oppressed people innovated arcane principles was both staggering and ominous. Further investigation led to the discovery that the onset of these powers coincided almost exactly with the Rivening. The first recorded instance of a human sorcerer was only three years after that fateful day when our priests went mad. The connection is, I believe, undeniable.

Decades of subsequent investigation unearthed evidence even more damning. Human occultists believe their most nefarious goddess, named Thamar, gave arcane power as a "gift" to her followers as a weapon to wield against the Orgoth. Even human priests insist this mysterious transaction left a taint on human souls. Research by arcanists, including those of House Vyre, further discovered tenuous clues that human magic exacerbates the fundamental cosmological dilemmas we suffer as a result of our missing gods. While the evidence is more suggestive than absolute, it seems increasingly likely the escalation of human arcane practices has increased the occurrence of soullessness, as one example. Additionally, similar studies conclude this corruptive influence extends to the proliferation of human mechanika as well as those who directly invoke magic. Awareness of this troubling pattern was the most important goad to prompt the movement that would eventually become the Retribution of Scyrah.

RISE OF THE SPLINTER SECTS

Two significant organizations emerged in response to the announcement of Scyrah's plight, the Retribution of Scyrah and the Seekers. The basic purpose of these sects was the same: take action where the Fane of Scyrah had stood paralyzed. For both groups the dire situation of our people required an immediate response. Where they differed was on the nature of that response.

While I do not deny my fundamental disagreements with Seeker philosophy, I admire their spirit. The group was founded with the intent of saving Scyrah from her doom. Much of their work is based on principles laid down two hundred and seventy years ago by a brilliant young diviner, Vyrillis Yryas. The Seekers have undeniably succeeded in collecting a wealth of historical and arcane lore, including tomes the Fane of Scyrah has declared forbidden that predate the Cataclysm. Yryas' heavy reliance on ancient texts and questionable prophecies, however, has led the Seekers to countless futile investigations and dead ends. Furthermore, they stubbornly reject the idea that human magic and the Rivening are linked.

Members of this organization cling to the hope that most of the Vanished still exist and are waiting to be found. The Seekers have made it their life's work to search beyond Ios for information pertinent to the recovery of the Vanished. A fundamental Seeker prophecy interprets a statement made by Lacyr to imply that Ios will someday require the help of outsiders to survive. Though they have achieved no notable gains in the last three centuries, the discovery of Nyssor has reinvigorated their cause. They insist he is only the first of several Vanished awaiting recovery.

By contrast the Retribution of Scyrah was founded on far more pragmatic principles. There is a strong religious foundation to the Retribution maintained by its dedicated priests and embodied by the pious mage hunters, yet at its core this organization is based on information gathered through research and reconnaissance. The Retribution has realized our only hope of restoring Scyrah is through the elimination of human magic and its practitioners. They have established hidden bases throughout the human kingdoms for use in the planning and execution of surgical strikes chosen to help slacken the noose around Scyrah's neck.

Not long after the official founding of the Retribution of Scyrah, the sect was outlawed and its membership declared unlawful. Similar sanctions fell on the Seekers, as the Consulate Court feared that such efforts could reveal the weakness of Ios and thereby invite invasion. Both the hallytyr and the Fane of Scyrah clearly hoped to quash these sects before they could take root, but numerous citizens had heard their call and devoted themselves to their causes. Sadly, a great portion of Ios' citizens were content to pretend that life would continue as it always had. As in the time of the Great Malaise, they distracted themselves with petty internal politics and inconsequential diversions.

THE FALL OF ISSYRAH

While other Iosan cities were lost to abandonment or the Rivening, the last to fall was Issyrah, destroyed by the dragon Ethrunbal in the year ^4356. Later reconstruction of events suggests Ethrunbal may have been hiding beneath the city for decades for its own enigmatic purposes.

The first sign of the dragon was when an abhorrent creature shambled out of the abandoned Fane of Ayisla to murder nearby citizens on the streets. Examination of its corpse revealed it had once been an Iosan and had been horrendously disfigured by blighted growths. This suggested the proximity of a dragon, which the Iosans knew from their contact with Rhul were tremendously destructive creatures.

Despite a prompt response from military forces gathered from the Gates of Mists and Storms, the Iosans entirely underestimated the scope of the threat. Rather than evacuate the city, the soldiery ventured into the tunnels below the fane to confront the dragon directly. Soon Ethrunbal erupted from beneath the earth to begin wholesale carnage. The creature laid waste to Issyrah and slaughtered thousands of its inhabitants. Eventually massed military forces put the dragon down, but only after suffering horrendous losses. Of the houses represented in the battle, House Rhyslyrr felt the death toll most keenly, losing almost an entire generation of soldiers to the dragon.

Iosan sages knew enough to extract the dragon's athanc, which they delivered far from their lands. Unknown to them, its chosen hiding place would be the undoing of their distant relatives the Nyss: Ethrunbal escaped his prison in ^4570 and spawned the Legion of Everblight.

RISE OF LORD GHYRRSHYLD

The human kingdoms rising to power after the Orgoth proved to be more amenable to our ambassadors and willing to conduct trade than their predecessors. During this period our mercantile houses were eager to broaden access to resources abroad. Their enthusiasm had to be kept in check by the Five Great Military Houses, who were prudently wary. Despite their objections some outsiders were even allowed to traverse our lands, but most trade was conducted at the Gate of Mists. Only a select few individuals were allowed to venture as far as Iryss.

The exiled sects continued their secret work, and Scyrah continued to weaken. For every human wizard or warcaster the mage hunters killed, three more emerged. In this time the Retribution of Scyrah began to speak of the Consulate Court with open disdain, and such opinions were echoed even in the halls of power. To many it seemed as if the government had become a morass of fruitless bickering and that nothing would change our predestined doom.

Even among the hallytyr some believed only great and decisive action would rouse the Iosan citizens from apathetic torpor. This was the stage set by ^4546 when a single leader stepped forward to challenge the status quo and eventually provoke civil war. This was Lord Ghyrrshyld, who rose to dominate House Vyre. His keen mind and forceful personality swept aside any opposition. He disbanded the incissar council ruling the house and declared himself Narcissar and High Consul of House Vyre. Even his

ETHRUNBAL RAZES ISSYRAH

opponents found his strength of will compelling. He was a leader who inspired hope at a time when inspiration was difficult to find.

This was not enough for Lord Ghyrrshyld. He intended to become a true narcissar, not just of house Vyre but of all Ios. "Emperor" is the literal meaning of the title, and it was his dream to embody that ideal. Lord Ghyrrshyld intended to force the people to confront our looming destruction. He knew the answer to our dilemma was not to be found inside our nation.

Ghyrrshyld possessed considerable occult knowledge and unsurpassed arcane skill. He had spent long years delving into the ancient archives of our learned house as well as tomes liberated from the libraries of House Shyeel. He was rumored to possess writings of the depraved cult of Nyrro and even lore purloined from Rhul as well as from the human wizards of Ceryl and Caspia. Without question his library included forbidden texts: stolen documents from Skell and Blackwater, a copy of the black pages of Thamar's Enkheiridion, and transcripts of tablets from the vanished kingdom humans call Morrdh. He disdained no knowledge, regardless of its source.

Whatever desperation impelled him, it sprang from a desire to restore our future. It was his belief Ios required a single unquestioned ruler like himself in order to find the path to salvation. This would lead to his growing conviction that our people's survival necessitated marshalling the might of Ios to expunge humanity entirely. Some have called him insane, but his madness reflected the dire plight of our people.

Many of the hallytyr maintained house soldiers, yet the degree to which High Consul Ghyrrshyld armed his kinsmen was unprecedented. Many Vyre nobles happily presumed Ghyrrshyld intended to transform our house into the sixth Great Military House. Others were less comfortable with apparent ascendancy, as we had always been a hallytyr of lore and arcane wisdom and reserved our soldiers for defense.

Steadily, dissenting voices among our nobles quieted and those in support became more vocal as Ghyrrshyld consolidated his absolute hold on the house. Many of our arcanists and technicians were eager to follow his lead, as it allowed them to practice uncommon arcane techniques and to strengthen our arsenal of myrmidons. The construction of these machines of war was an esteemed specialty, but House Vyre had traditionally been overshadowed by our Shyeel rivals.

Ghyrrshyld tested the forces at his disposal in battle regularly, and it was not long before all his officers knew his preference for spilling blood by his own hand. Several surviving letters and journals contain descriptions of him returning to his army encampments drenched in gore, as though each battle were a sacrificial baptism. No enemy escaped his blade, but he targeted primitive trollkin inhabiting the region south of Mount Shyleth Breen particularly. I have no strong sympathy for these brutes—they are a warlike and bloodthirsty species—but certainly they had done nothing to invite such assailment.

It is no surprise that in the aftermath of these attacks a sizable number of trollkin tribes banded together to seek vengeance. It was a foolish and ill-conceived notion, but in their ignorance they did not know what they faced. Lord Ghyrrshyld met them at the fore of his army. The resulting slaughter did much to feed the dark rumors surrounding the narcissar of House Vyre.

Away from battle he was an eloquent orator, seeming to possess that rare balance of wisdom and fervor that kindles empathy in the hardest heart. I heard his stirring speeches firsthand and felt the desire to please him myself. His subordinates were all devoted. It seemed little matter to them that he was cruel in war, for what is war but cruelty itself? Ghyrrshyld's excesses were seen as confirmation of a virile and passionate leader.

Events took a far darker turn in ^4547. Lysevyn, wife of Ghyrrshyld's cousin and much beloved within the house, gave birth to a soulless child in Shyrr. Much hope had been placed on the birth, as few children of the direct lineage of Vyre had been born in several decades. It is said that when he heard the ill tidings Ghyrrshyld rushed into the birthing chamber, his eyes filled with rage. As the exhausted mother wept and screamed at him, he tore the babe from her breast and stormed away. The infant made no noise, as the soulless are silent at birth, but stared up at its kinsman blankly.

Without pause High Consul Ghyrrshyld Vyre barged into the chamber of the Consulate Court where a partial assembly had gathered to discuss matters of law. Before their horrified eyes Ghyrrshyld held the soulless child aloft as he decried the failings of the court in the face of certain doom. He challenged them to ignore the facts in front of their eyes. Without warning, he dashed the skull of the child on the stone floor at their feet. His raving became more intense as he demanded they heed his call to march to war, to set loose their blades to avenge the goddess even unto their last breath. Eventually his own retinue pulled the narcissar from the chamber, erupting the Consulate Court into chaos.

So shocking was this display that it took some time for the ambivalent consuls to take action. Ghyrrshyld and most of House Vyre retreated to Iryss and sealed our ancestral gates, refusing all inquiries. The other consuls issued an arrest warrant for Narcissar Ghyrrshyld Vyre and demanded he return to the capital and submit to their authority. When agents made these demands at the gates of the Vyre demesne they were warned they had but one chance to depart. When they insisted Lord Ghyrrshyld be surrendered, the Vyre houseguard opened fire. Thus began the War of the Houses.

THE WAR OF THE HOUSES

What at first seemed an isolated conflict soon escalated into wider hostilities. House Vyre quickly succeeded in rallying the nobles of Iryss against the apparent tyranny of the Consulate Court. The other hallytyr did not understand the depth of Ghyrrshyld's absolute control over his house and certainly did not expect the extent of his alliances with numerous lesser houses, each eager to change their fortunes by this sudden opportunity. The degree to which House Vyre had prepared and armed itself for this eventuality took his enemies completely unaware. Arrogance was partially at fault, as the Five Great Military Houses could not imagine anyone—much less a lone house—with the strength to confront them. After the defeat of a dragon at Issyrah, the military might of a single hallytyr seemed trivial.

Before anyone realized the severity of the threat, Lord Ghyrrshyld and his army brazenly marched to Shyrr. Ghyrrshyld's intimate knowledge of the city and its defenses was a significant factor in his initial success, an advantage no foreign invader could have hoped to replicate. The sheer magnitude of myrmidons fielded by this army was also unexpected, and it remains unclear how and where these were manufactured. It seems inescapable there was collaboration from within Shyrr by those enamored of Ghyrrshyd's peculiar genius.

The most audacious move in the initial attack was the manner in which Ghyrrshyld tied up the forces of House Silowuyr, the sworn defenders of the capital. A sizable contingent of Vyre riflemen and heavy myrmidons laid siege to the capital garrison. It was surrounded and cut off, forcing defenders elsewhere in the city to rally and converge in an attempt to break the siege. Meanwhile Ghyrrshyld and a company of heavily armored escorts marched directly to the Consulariat. The consuls of the hallytyr stood paralyzed as the self-declared Narcissar of Ios took them hostage.

Key to Ghyrrshyld's plan, the capital's heavy fortifications and concentric defenses were designed to grant a smaller force of defenders the advantage against a larger invading force. Because of this, once entrenched the army of House Vyre was able to hold the center of Shyrr for weeks. Within the consulariat itself, despite their captivity the heads of the hallytyr resolutely refused to acknowledge Ghyrrshyld as their master. The Vyre High Consul was determined to force their submission and for that reason alone kept them alive through the ordeal, although their treatment at his hands was far from gentle.

House Silowuyr proved tenacious, its garrison enduring siege with few casualties, but it could not break loose. This occupied a substantial portion of Vyre's army and gave Houses Nyarr and Ellowuyr the chance to muster their forces from the Aeryth Dawnguard and Aeryth Ellowuyr, respectively. House Shyeel contributed its support and sent its own forces, including several dozens of formidable myrmidons, to march alongside the Dawnguard.

The ensuing clash in southern Shyrr was bloody but relatively brief, as the Vyre army quickly realized its untenable position. It seems likely Lord Ghyrrshyld would have executed all the consuls if not for a bold attack by a handpicked team assembled by House Silowuyr. These courageous soldiers sacrificed themselves in a desperate attack on the central chamber that drew the defenders into pitched battle so the consuls could be rescued and taken to safety. With additional forces threatening their position, Vyre's generals persuaded their enraged lord to withdraw. A fighting retreat to Iryss began two long years of conflict that gradually drew in additional houses until the war touched every corner of Ios. By its end several substantial houses had been obliterated and countless lives ruined, each death an avoidable tragedy.

Two of our Five Great Military Houses stood conspicuously absent from the conflict. House Rhyslyrr had suffered badly in the fall of Issyrah and their soldiers were entrusted with the Gate of Mists. It is understandable that they could not put aside their southern vigil to quell internal strife. There has never been an entirely satisfactory explanation, however, for the absence of House Issyen. Some suggest Issyen collaborated with Vyre during the civil war, but definitive proof has never been offered.

Ghyrrshyld remained defiant and insisted he fought only to unite Ios and to cure our people, yet during those two years he and his soldiers secretly gathered hundreds of infants to subject them to cruel testing and experiments, all on the excuse of seeking a solution to the soulless dilemma. The number of children killed in these experiments can never be confirmed—and must be admitted as subject to exaggeration—but it seems likely upward of a thousand were slain. Our people are still coming to grips with the horrors instigated at this time, as the wanton murder of innocent children is all the more atrocious in a time when such births are so infrequent.

The Retribution of Scyrah was not directly involved until the end of the conflict. It must be remembered that the organization was outlawed within Ios. Many of its best warriors were in exile fighting their secret battles on human soil. Among the populace, ignorance sometimes confused Ghyrrshyld's rhetoric with the Retribution's cause, and the sect's leadership worried about being tainted by this mistaken association.

House Shyeel was the first to discover the scope of Ghyrrshyld's atrocities in late ^4548, impelling the alliance against House Vyre to act with greater urgency. In the opening months of the next year, the allied houses committed to a full assault on Iryss led by the Dawnguard and myrmidons of House Shyeel. The hallytyr had previously avoided such a battle in the hopes of sparing that sacred city any substantial destruction. All involved were sensitive to the relevance of this city to Scyrah. Even as the assault drove forward, the alliance made what efforts it could to protect the Fane of Scyrah and other holy sites.

For this final push Houses Nyarr and Shyeel convinced the Retribution to lend its assistance, a fact largely overlooked until now. All nearby forces the Retribution could muster joined an assault against the heart of House Vyre. I was among those who aided in this attack, putting aside my house loyalties to help Retribution mage hunters penetrate Vyre's protective wards. Invictor rifle fire and Shyeel battle mage blasts tore asunder ancient stones laid down by the first generation of the survivors of the Lyossan Empire as the forces led by the Dawnguard picked apart the once-mighty army of House Vyre.

The attackers triumphed, but Ghyrrshyld denied them the satisfaction of his capture or death. Dawnlord Vyros Nyarr confronted the narcissar in the chambers below the estates. Neither of them emerged unscathed from the ensuing duel. Vyros mortally injured Ghyrrshyld, but the narcissar's bodyguard interceded and bought enough time for the former high consul to escape through hidden and extensively trapped passages. With Ghyrrshyld driven away and dying of his wounds, the rest of the Vyre army surrendered. The war was over.

House Vyre has suffered much in the intervening decades, which I do not consider unjust. All those discovered to have knowingly collaborated in Ghyrrshyld's deeper depravities were executed. For a time the complete disintegration of the house was considered; it was a drastic step, but many leaders felt it to be the one response that could be made in the face of such horrific acts. Only the impassioned pleas of our most senior scholars and nobles convinced the Consulate Court that service over millennia should not be forgotten by the misdeeds of so few, however grave.

I believe it is from guilt over this period that many members of House Vyre have taken up the Seekers' cause or devoted their efforts to the Fane of Scyrah. Others like myself have answered the call of the Retribution.

It would be years before any of us would learn of Ghyrrshyld's fate, and we still do not know most of the details of his flight. It is evident that sometime after his battle with Dawnlord Vyros, Ghyrrshyld became an unliving abomination. Clearly he possessed the lore to transform himself into an eldritch, those most unholy creatures connected to the corrupt priests of Nyrro. Perhaps he resorted to this to escape death by his injuries, or perhaps he chose it more willingly; we will never know for certain. We do know he took refuge where the dead are welcomed, in the Nightmare Empire of Cryx. Even after the identity of the eldritch serving Cryx was discerned by agents abroad decades later, it is doubtful anyone expected this creature might yet have a part to play in the fate of our people.

REFUSAL OF THE NYSS EMISSARIES

One significant event in the history of Ios has gone largely unrecognized and undiscussed. Shortly after the return of Scyrah, several Nyss elders arrived at the Gate of Mists requesting ingress and claiming they had vital information for the Fane of Scyrah. These Nyss had travelled very far and endured hardships to reach their destination but were greeted with rude disregard. The guardians of the gates were in a state of high alert, their vigil taken to almost paranoid heights by the recent return of the divine presence. The arrival of those who represented the long-absent and self-exiled sect of the god of winter was not welcomed.

Unbeknownst to anyone in Ios these emissaries had been sent on the orders of Nyssor himself and bore information for the Fane of Scyrah related to the plight of the goddess. The god of winter had conveyed these instructions before his own ailment forced him to encase himself in ice for self-preservation. After repeated attempts at admittance, the Nyss emissaries reluctantly turned away and repeated the trek back to the Shard Spires. From this point forward the Nyss considered themselves irrevocably sundered from their Iosan cousins. The exact contents of Nyssor's message were subsequently lost. Only a few among the Seekers sect have even the slightest clues related to this missed opportunity.

LEGACY OF DARSAEL

At the outset of the War of the Houses, all Iosan ambassadors had been recalled and the gates sealed against outsiders. An already cautious policy toward other nations became absolute isolation. Ios was closed. These measures prevented the human nations from learning of the civil strife and the general degradation of Iosan cities and security, but a closed Ios does nothing to improve hope for Scyrah's recovery.

In most respects nothing significant has changed in these last thirty years since the War of the Houses, which is perhaps the greatest tragedy of Ghyrrshyld's legacy. Soulless children continued to be born and quietly killed or sometimes smuggled into Retribution hands. The message Ghyrrshyld had gone to such lengths to deliver was forgotten—until contact with forgotten relations brought a rude awakening.

With so much else to occupy our attention little time or effort has been spent examining the lives of our distant cousins, the Nyss. It has been over 22 hecyion since the former inhabitants of Darsael heeded the call to follow the prophet

Aeric and march into the far northern mountains. From what little I understand of their culture, I can say it bears almost no resemblance to ours. Living hand-to-mouth as hunters and nomads regressed their ways in some respects, and they lost the literacy of our tongue to adopt a simpler and cruder language. Even their bodies no longer seem the same; generations in the forsaken and frozen peaks have made them alien to us.

Were it not for the intelligence gathered by members of the Retribution of Scyrah and Seekers working outside Ios, it is entirely possible no one in Ios would even have known the descendants of Darsael still existed, so small was their impact. Even after becoming aware of the Nyss, we disregarded them as a small and insignificant offshoot of our people who had voluntarily abandoned the safety of our borders and our civilization alike. Recent events have changed everything. Only now, when it may be too late, have we started to grasp the ramifications of our ignorance. In retrospect we should never have lost touch with these people or disregarded their claims that they were chosen by the Scyir of Winter.

Only a few years ago the Nyss suffered complete upheaval. With no warning their communities were beset by hostile invaders disfigured with similar blight as witnessed before the fall of Issyrah. The tribes fought as they could but were forced to flee the Shard Spires of northern Khador. We have only recently begun to speak with refugees of this attack, working as we can to overcome language and cultural barriers. The stories are disoriented and fragmentary, yet it seems increasingly likely the force attacking them must have been sent and led by Ethrunbal. The dragon that annihilated Issyrah and which we thought sealed and forgotten has arisen again.

Hidden Retribution cells near Korsk were the first to investigate this tragedy, and what they perceived would forever change the future of our people. It was Eiryss, Angel of Retribution, who discovered a secret the Nyss must have been maintaining for centuries. At some point after the Rivening, Nyssor had apparently returned to his chosen people just as Scyrah had returned to Ios. The Nyss fleeing the forces of Ethrunbal had carried the god concealed among them, hoping to keep his divinity safe from those who followed after.

Eiryss learned the ailing Nyssor had sheathed himself in ice as a means to slow his degeneration. The Nyss had sought to protect his frozen body further by encasing it in stone inscribed with holy sigils. They had conveyed this vault with them into the heart of Khador. In an attempt to conceal the god from the forces that had largely destroyed their people, Nyssor's priests secreted this vault below Korsk's greatest holy structure and there attended him night and day. The Khadorans knew nothing of the significance of this massive block of stone but that their holy men had agreed to offer sanctuary to the Nyss priests and their enigmatic burden.

It is a particular tragedy that these refugees did not immediately come to Ios for protection but rather sought shelter among those who would later betray them. Perhaps to a people so long sundered from civilization Korsk seemed well protected and secure from threat. Had Ios maintained closer relations with the Nyss, perhaps they would have chosen to return home. Alas, that event did not come to pass.

Eiryss at once apprehended the importance of such a finding. This at last was evidence of the survival of one of the Vanished! If the news was true, it meant Nyssor might be returned to Ios and could assist with Scyrah's divine burden. Wishing to verify the claim with her own eyes, Eiryss made her way to the human cathedral.

It is impossible not to conclude the close timing of this mission involved divine providence. As Eiryss arrived at the outer door of the cathedral, she found its guards slaughtered. Within its depths she eventually stumbled upon Nyssor's shattered stone vault. There she witnessed the Scyir of Winter, partially thawed from his frozen rest, being attacked by a nightmare creature. This was none other than the eldritch Goreshade, who had once been Lord Ghyrrshyld of House Vyre. This unholy creature had stolen Nyssor's sword Voass and profaned it with his touch. His unholy hands proved too feeble to slay a god with a single blow, and the sound of approaching defenders prompted Goreshade to flee the chamber.

Eiryss pursued the eldritch from the cathedral in hopes of striking him down, but fighting him alone she was no more successful than Dawnlord Vyros had been three decades earlier. Goreshade dealt Eiryss a crippling injury but withheld the deathblow, allowing her to live to pass on word of his deeds. By her testimony it would seem this creature retains the mad belief that he holds the secret of our salvation, toward which he is willing to commit any blasphemy. His incomprehensible plan will lead to the extinction of our people as well as our remaining gods.

Left bleeding in the streets of Korsk, Eiryss gathered her waning strength to return to Nyssor to try to ameliorate the damage Goreshade's blasphemy had done. There she witnessed another equally terrible profanity. Khadoran soldiers had assembled at the cathedral with members of the Greylords Covenant, the wizards of that nation. They had secured the god's vault and were preparing it for transport.

Knowing others must be told what she had seen, the injured Eiryss risked her life hastening back to Ios. The gravity of her news stunned the Consulate Court and the Fane of Scyrah both: One of our gods has been found. All evidence suggests Nyssor is captive, held by a most hated enemy. Furthermore, Eiryss' description of Goreshade's words had made it clear our gods are not safe from humanity, nor the Nightmare Empire, nor the dragon Ethrunbal. Swift action is required lest Nyssor's fate be sealed and he is lost to us forever.

WHAT TOMORROW BRINGS

These events have both electrified and terrified our people, awakening them like plunging into an icy river. At last the words of the Retribution of Scyrah have reached ears formerly closed to them. No one can ignore the very real peril human wizardry represents to our gods. With this news, the Retribution has at last been able to step from the shadows. Our agents have been instrumental in returning the Nyss to Ios. Reuniting with our lost cousins has been a great boon, as we have dire need of the secrets they hold.

Houses Nyarr and Shyeel have once again proven their commitment, stepping forward immediately to support the Retribution and placing their own reputations at stake. They have brought with them tremendous military assets by which we have a chance to recover Nyssor from the hands of our enemies. A long and difficult struggle lies ahead of us, as we are outnumbered many hundreds to one. But this is not a time for hesitation or caution. Scyrah lies dying in Shyrr; Nyssor is captive of human wizards; and the eldritch Goreshade plots to instigate the swift annihilation of our few remaining gods.

Whatever hope we may find in discovering the survival of Nyssor, we must seize it now. The next few years will be vital in determining whether we will endure to bring another generation into this world. For the sake of our children— indeed, of our very souls!—we must march to war. It is not hatred that motivates us, but hope. Let the knowledge of the cost of failure lend a wild and savage strength to our cause so that we may rise again as a proud and valiant people worthy of our legacy.

MILITARY OF IOS
AND THE RETRIBUTION OF SCYRAH

The organization of the armed forces committed to the Retribution of Scyrah is evolving as its leaders guide the sect through a massive transition. Not long ago the Retribution was an outlawed fringe organization of zealous and violent fanatics. Their goal has always been the eradication of human wizards and sorcerers, whom they hold responsible for the ills of their species. Until recently they have had to work in secrecy from numerous cells within neighboring human kingdoms. Now things have changed. Their message has found a voice inside Ios and they have won new allies to their cause. They are no longer forced to hide their affiliations and have begun to organize into an army capable of waging open warfare. Though the Retribution represents a minority in Ios, it is growing rapidly—and recent events promise to bring even more converts. The Retribution is now large and influential enough to abandon secrecy at home and to become a recognized political, religious, and military power.

The Retribution has gained access to a significant portion of the armed might of the nation, including hundreds of myrmidons and the Dawnguard legions of House Nyarr, who are among Ios' most formidable warriors. While their size and the scope of their military capability has increased nearly a hundredfold from what it was, their army remains relatively small compared to the nations against which they plan to strike. They are also competing for resources inside Ios with the force assigned to defend the nation's borders, collectively referred to as the Homeguard Coalition.

This has prompted the Retribution to adopt unconventional strategies, including a unique doctrine of engagement. They wield their forces like a spear set against the weakest point in the armor of their enemies. Comprehensive reconnaissance combined with rapid redeployment is the key to Retribution strategy. Their forces are uniquely equipped to wage this type of warfare and thereby represent a threat far greater than numbers alone may suggest.

Working to the Retribution's advantage is the fact that the human kingdoms know little about them while their own intelligence-gathering efforts have been thorough. Ios has not been involved in any significant external war in its entire history, largely due to its prolonged policy of isolationism and its fearsome reputation for protecting its borders. Some might expect this means Iosan soldiers are inexperienced at waging war, but the military has enforced extensive training and discipline to keep the nation at constant martial readiness throughout its existence. Several internal clashes unknown to the outside world have additionally helped hone their fighting prowess. The true reason Ios sealed its borders in 581 AR was to conceal the onset of a brutal and bloody civil war. This War of the Houses left a lasting legacy, and many Iosan soldiers are veterans of the conflict.

The resolve of Iosan soldiers is strengthened by the knowledge that they fight for their survival as a species. They intend to strike against enemies thought to have played a hand in the extinction of their gods. At their core they remain a fiercely dedicated and religiously charged organization that now has access to a powerful and sophisticated armory as well as sufficient soldiers to wage war against humanity.

A MILITARY DIVIDED

There is a significant distinction between the Retribution military and the forces serving the Iosan government. The rise of the Retribution has divided and placed additional strains on the Homeguard Coalition, the collective army sworn to defend the borders of Ios. Furthermore, there are considerable differences among the warriors of the Retribution itself: its soldiers are not all of one mind or purpose, nor do they recognize the same chain of command.

THE HOMEGUARD COALITION

For centuries Ios' unassailable borders have been supervised by five of the *hallytyr*, or "high houses." These are the Five Great Military Houses of Ios: Ellowuyr, Issyen, Nyarr, Rhyslyrr, and Silowuyr. Each is responsible for overseeing a key Iosan fortress as well as contributing to border patrols and interior garrisons. A complex arrangement of rotating personnel has become a regular part of Iosan military custom as soldiers periodically relocate to posts around the realm. Each house has its own practices and specialties, but these forces as a whole are called the Homeguard Coalition. Led by the Five Great Military Houses, the Homeguard also includes soldiers drawn from the ranks of dozens of lesser houses who collectively share responsibility for the defense of Ios.

In theory the Iosan army practices voluntary enlistment, but in practice many individuals succumb to pressure to enlist in order to meet their social obligations or increase their opportunities for advancement. Officer commissions within the Homeguard Coalition are considered lucrative and socially advantageous careers, and such a background is essential for Iosans seeking higher station. Military service is divided into 10-year increments. It is common for young elves from any background to enlist for at least a single term. A smaller number enlist repeatedly, possibly becoming career soldiers.

Enlistment is widespread at both extremes of the social stratum for different reasons. Poor families encourage sons or daughters to enlist because it removes them as a strain on family resources and allows them to improve their family standing. Some may return a portion of their military wages to their kin. Members of the affluent houses, particularly the Five Great Military Houses, are expected to serve several terms of service to learn skills considered essential to their leadership roles. Many noble sons and daughters not being groomed as heirs become career soldiers regardless of other skills or talents. The lesser houses beholden to the hallytyr are expected to do their part to help fill the ranks. A variety of political and social pressures can be brought to bear on them to ensure this. It is not uncommon for family pressures to require a soldier to serve at least one or two terms before being released to pursue outside avocations.

This system has helped ensure a sufficient standing army, but it also means its soldiers are not equally diligent or skilled. The Homeguard Coalition arguably suffers from

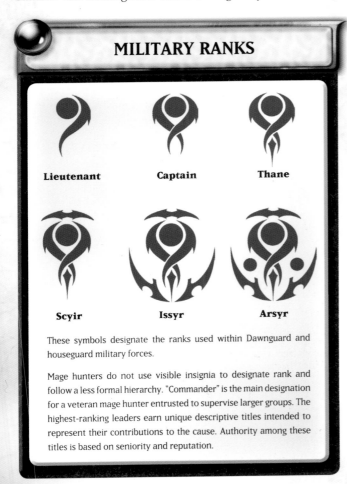

MILITARY RANKS

Lieutenant   Captain   Thane

Scyir   Issyr   Arsyr

These symbols designate the ranks used within Dawnguard and houseguard military forces.

Mage hunters do not use visible insignia to designate rank and follow a less formal hierarchy. "Commander" is the main designation for a veteran mage hunter entrusted to supervise larger groups. The highest-ranking leaders earn unique descriptive titles intended to represent their contributions to the cause. Authority among these titles is based on seniority and reputation.

opportunists and inept officers focused on securing safe and lucrative posts. The officers from the Five Great Military Houses, however, are among the nation's best trained and dedicated, as their standing in their houses is inextricably tied to their records of service. The guiding hands of these professionals has served to maintain the overall quality of the Coalition despite the inadequacies of some of their peers.

While each of the Five Great Military Houses has a well-rounded military force, they all have notable specialties as well. For example, House Nyarr is known for its heavy infantry trained to fight closely alongside myrmidons. House Ellowuyr boasts Ios' most renowned and tactically aggressive swordsmen. House Issyen takes pride in its famed cavalry, intended to be able to move rapidly to any threatened region of the border. House Rhyslyrr is known for the accuracy of both its archers and its riflemen. House Silowuyr's pious and ritualistic soldiers are oath-sworn to protect the Iosan capital of Shyrr to the last.

The largest standing border garrison guards the Gate of Mists, the great southwestern fortress serving as the entry point to Ios proper. A sizable secondary garrison keeps watch to the north at the Gate of Storms which faces the Rhulic border. Ios has never had a major conflict with Rhul but has kept this fortress heavily manned regardless. While the placement of the Aeryth Dawnguard has made its defenses less relevant to western threats, it was originally built to guard Ios' eastern border against any enemies that might follow across the wastes. Given recent increases in skorne activity, this fortress stands at constant alert. Even while the majority of the Dawnguard have marched to join the Retribution, a strong reserve garrison remains here.

The largest interior garrison is Aeryth Ellowuyr, a massive training fortress that helps forge houseguard from assorted backgrounds into cohesive companies. There is also a sizable garrison directly protecting Shyrr; House Silowuyr leads this force, which also includes a select honor guard with members from each of the Five Great Military Houses. Smaller barracks exist throughout Ios, including in the cities of Iryss and Lynshynal. Over the last two decades, the ruling council authorized the construction of a chain of smaller border fortresses that now connect the major garrisons and support patrols.

Myrmidons accompany border patrols primarily composed of infantry and cavalry. Bolstering the patrols are the surveillance efforts provided by diviners within the Homeguard Coalition who watch the nation's borders. These diviners employ a variety of arcanik scrying devices in their work, making it very difficult for outsiders to violate the Iosan border without drawing immediate notice and brutal reprisal.

The Homeguard Coalition has changed in the wake of the Retribution's mobilization but remains superficially intact.

POLITICS AND RELIGION IN IOS

Religion is an unavoidable fact of Iosan politics, as it has been since the inception of the nation. When Ios was created, the eight gods of the Divine Court walked among the citizens; it was natural they would be integrated into the government of the new nation. The Divine Court is the highest authority in the land, above the Consulate Court. Although the gods left governance to mortals and rarely invoked this privilege even when they were still present, the laws investing that authority remain.

After the departure of the gods these laws were expanded to apply to Iosan clergy. The ranking priests of the fanes were invited to represent the Divine Court in the Consulate Court where they exercised considerable influence. When the Rivening toppled the other fanes, this function fell exclusively to the Fane of Scyrah. Members of the Auricyl Velahn, Scyrah's leading priests, freely attend the Consulate Court, and their words still hold considerable sway.

With the Retribution's recent rise to prominence, its priests have been petitioning for identical recognition. Oracle Relvinor Luynmyr has demanded the right to participate as a representative of Scyrah on the Consulate Court. The Fane of Scyrah has vehemently objected, but the matter is undecided. This concession seems a matter of time. Should it come to pass it would further legitimize the entire sect in the mind of the average Iosan citizen.

The fact that one of the Five Great Military Houses has openly embraced the Retribution cause has roused great turmoil in political circles but has had less immediate impact on border defenses. Aeryth Dawnguard, House Nyarr's primary fortress, has always been geographically remote; its elite Dawnguard was never a major part of southern border patrols, so their recent absence has had little real impact. Consul Caelcyr Nyarr has vowed that a small force of his soldiers will still help guard Shyrr and that House Nyarr will maintain other major garrisons, but fully two-thirds of its active soldiers now march openly in the service of the Retribution.

Of graver concern to the other military houses is the fact that House Shyeel has pledged its support—and more importantly, its myrmidon reserves and future production—to the Retribution. Although House Shyeel is not technically a military house, it is the foremost producer of Iosan warjacks. The house has a virtual monopoly on the most advanced myrmidon arcanika and has a particularly strong hold on manufacturing. In addition to providing support personnel, Shyeel has dispatched several warcasters to serve the Retribution cause.

The house's largest rival in this industry is House Vyre, which hopes to increase its own standing by filling military contracts abandoned by Shyeel. This will take time, though, as House Vyre's production facilities are considerably smaller than those of House Shyeel. The Consulate Court

fears an overt attack by a foreign power could exploit this weakness. Leaders of the Retribution insist they will fight to guarantee such an eventuality never comes to pass, but their assurances seem hollow. House Shyeel has turned a deaf ear to entreaties to institute an equitable division of military resources.

In addition to the impact of the withdrawal of these two hallytyr, Retribution recruitment has taken its toll on the force strength of the homeguard. The remaining four military houses have expressed concern that the Retribution's rising popularity could reduce their numbers to unacceptable levels. For now the border remains secure, but it has yet to be seriously tested. With the Retribution escalating hostilities abroad it seems inevitable its enemies will eventually bring the fight to Ios, and the worst fears of the Consulate Court might be realized. Despite this, the human nations and Rhul have always considered Ios' borders impregnable, and this reputation may serve where strength of arms alone would not.

AN ARMY NOT OF THE STATE

For now the Retribution of Scyrah exists amid considerable political tension and unrest. Relations with the government and the Homeguard Coalition are far from comfortable. Bolstered by the support of House Nyarr and House Shyeel, the Retribution recently seized the initiative and forced the Consulate Court to recognize its standing. The government felt compelled to acknowledge the Retribution as a lawful organization, but none of the other hallytyr are pleased with the outcome.

HOUSE LEADERSHIP

Historically when a single leader led a house he or she assumed the title "Narcissar" in homage to Narcissar Lacyr. After the recent civil war, that title fell out of favor as it was associated with Narcissar Ghyrrshyld of House Vyre. Whether they lead alone or as part of a council, most house leaders today utilize the slightly humbler "Incissar" title. This derives from the god Ossyris, the Incissar of Hours, Sovereign of Conflict, and General of Lyoss, and has the additional advantage of representing a top military rank. This is appropriate as incissars are the top-ranking leaders of their house armies, whether or not they spend time in uniform directing the soldiers.

"Consul" is a special title afforded to a leading representative of each hallytyr appointed to attend the Consulate Court and speak for the house in matters of state. Most consuls have also been narcissars or incissars. The leaders of a hallytyr can freely nominate any of their peers to sit on the Consulate Court, including senior advisors or politically adept relations. Most enjoy the authority they wield as consuls, however, and are unwilling to surrender the post to anyone else unless compelled by other duties, age, or illness.

IOSAN GOVERNMENT
AND THE RETRIBUTION MILITARY

Major Iosan Religious Sects

DIVINE COURT
Scyrah, Regent Narcissar • Nis-Issyr of Spring

VACANT SEATS

Lacyr, Narcissar of Ages
Ayisla, Nis-Arsyr of Night
Lurynsar, Issyr of Summer
Nyssor, Scyir of Winter

Ossyris, Incissar of Hours
Nyrro, Arsyr of Day
Lyliss, Nis-Scyir of Autumn

FANE OF SCYRAH
Led by the Eight Auricants
of the Auricyl Velahn
Majority Faith

RETRIBUTION PRIESTHOOD
Led by Oracle Relvinor Luynmyr
(Disreputable Sect)

THE SEEKERS
Master Diviner Vyrillis Yryas
Opener of Seals Myasuyrin
(Disreputable Sect)

CONSULATE COURT
Comprising the 15 Hallytyr High Houses

10 ADMINISTRATIVE AND GOVERNING HALLYTYR

AIESYN	EYVREYN	LYS	RYVRESE	SHYEEL
Construction	Lore, History	Physickers, Funerary Rites	Trade, Crafts	Myrmidons, Arcanika
Consul Klyvahn Aiesyn	Consul Darshyld Eyvreyn	Consul Mylita Lys	Consul Callis Ryvrese	Consul Hyselle Shyeel
SYLLRYNAL	**UITHUYR**	**VYRE**	**WYSHANALYRR**	**YRRYEL**
Agriculture	Education, Theology	Occult, Arcane Lore	Philosophy, Mathematics	Trade, Commerce
Consul Ashlor Syllrynal	Consul Darshyld Eyvreyn	Consul Alyssa Vyre	Consul Gehes Wyshanalyrr	Consul Maevryn Yrryel

THE FIVE GREAT MILITARY HOUSES

ELLOWUYR	ISSYEN	NYARR	RHYSLYRR	SILOWUYR
Aeryth Ellowuyr	Gate of Storms	Aeryth Dawnguard	Gate of Mists	Protects Shyrr
Consul Brysor Ellowuyr	Consul Jylvan Issyen	Consul Caelcyr Nyarr	Consul Iolas Rhyslyrr	Consul Garlryo Silowuyr

IOSAN HOMEGUARD COALITION
Led by the Five Great Military Houses
60,000 Soldiers (+ reserves)
Garrisons in each city, border fortress,
and military house stronghold

NINE VOICES OF THE RETRIBUTION
Consul Caelcyr Nyarr, Military Consul
Consul Hyselle Shyeel, Arcane Consul
Glyssor Syviis, Retribution Coordinator, Shyrr
Jarmyr of Eyvreyn, Annals Keeper
Kelsyr Yrryel, Espionage Liaison
Nyr Voshan, Retribution Quaestor
Oracle Relvinor Luynmyr, Ranking Retribution Priest
Orator Lysenne Bylvesh, First Aide to Relvinor
Keldeacon Synvas Uithuyr, Recruitment Coordinator

Military Operational Oversight

DAWNGUARD
House Nyarr's
standing army
Dawnguard: 4,000
Dawnlord Vyross Nyarr

SHYEEL FORCES
**Battle Mages: 300
Arcanists/Support:
1,000
Myrmidons:
Variable, 200+**
Adeptis Rahn Shyeel

HOUSEGUARD
Numerous houses
**Soldiers: 20,000
(and rising)
Support: 4,000+**
Houseguard Arsyr Norcyl
Various ranking officers

EXTERNAL CELLS
Bases outside Ios for
recon and resupply
**Mage Hunters: 900
Other: 200 (priests,
soulless, support, etc.)**
Ravyn, Eternal Light

SYVASH STRONGHOLD
Training and reserve
facility in Iryss
**Reserves: 400+
Staff: 50**
Keldeacon Synvas Uithuyr

CELL OPERATIONAL REGIONS — HQ
Caspia & Southern Cygnar — Mirror Armory
Korsk & Central Khador — Lynvass Hold
Ord — Myshen Enclave
Occupied Llael — Nylen Retreat
Ceryl & Western Cygnar — Ossian Armory
Northern Cygnar — Scylith Enclave
Southern Khador — Hylyssin Fasthold
Northern Khador — Jascyr Bunker

PRIMARY STRIKE ARMY
"Talons of Dawn"
Primary ready army
**Strength: Varies (first priority)
Current Theater: Khador
Goal: Recover Nyssor**
Dawnlord Vyross Nyarr
Ravyn, Eternal Light

SECONDARY STRIKE ARMY
"Scyrah's Blade"
Secondary ready army
**Strength: Varies
Current Theater:
Eastern Llael
Goal: Expand Iosan border**
Dawnlord Cyrsyll Nyarr
Adeptis Rahn Shyeel

ANCILLARY STRIKE TEAMS
"The Unseen Spear"
Supplemental to primary
and secondary armies
**Strength: Varies
Current Theater: Varies
Goal: Varies**
Dawnguard Issyr Rylavos Nyarr
Kaelyssa, Night's Whisper

PRIMARY VAN
**Dawnguard:
up to 3,000
Battle Mages:
up to 150
Myrmidons: 50 (heavy)**
Dawnguard Issyr
Osrhyar Nyarr

PRIMARY LINE
Veteran houseguard
**Houseguard: 10,000
Myrmidons: 60 (light)**
Houseguard Issyr Falwyn Lys

PRIMARY SPECIAL OPERATIONS
**Mage Hunters: 400
Myrmidons: 10-20**
Ravyn, Eternal Light

SCYRAH'S BLADE VAN
**Dawnguard:
up to 800
Battle Mages:
up to 80
Myrmidons: 20 (heavy)**
Dawnguard Issyr Lascyra Nyarr

SCYRAH'S BLADE LINE
Veteran houseguard
**Houseguard: 8,000
Myrmidons: 60 (light)**
Houseguard Issyr Aerin Mashyl

SCYRAH'S BLADE SPECIAL OPERATIONS
**Mage Hunters: 300
Myrmidons: 5-10**
Garryth, Blade of Retribution

VAN COMPANIES
**Infantry Companies: 15
Infantry per: 150
Cavalry Companies: 6
Cavalry per: 50**
Dawnguard Captains or Thanes

LINE COMPANIES
**Infantry Companies: 25
Soldiers per: 300
Cavalry Companies: 10
Cavalry per: 50**
Houseguard Captains or Thanes

STRIKE FORCES (5-20)
Leadership varies

MIXED COMPANIES (10)
**Infantry per: 50-150
Cavalry per: 0-50
Myrmidons per: 0-3**
Captains, Thanes, or Scyir

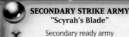

Most consuls gave their grudging acceptance after realizing that behind the Retribution's lofty rhetoric about Scyrah's fate lurked the threat of violence. Memories of the recent civil war are still fresh, and the consuls had no desire to see Ios torn apart again by internal strife. Lacking the will to oppose the Retribution with force, the consuls had no choice but to accept it as a valid political and military entity—one they agreed could act with minimal Consulate oversight. Technically the consuls of House Nyarr and House Shyeel are held responsible for the actions of the Retribution, but given their political views it is only an illusion of restraint.

The Consulate Court may have been forced to accept the existence of the Retribution, but it does not endorse or support the organization; the Retribution is not a state-sponsored force. Such an army, like those of Ios' neighboring kingdoms, would serve as a direct extension of the will of its sovereign. Although the Retribution does not act for Ios as a whole, humanity will likely see no distinction between the two and is expected to hold the nation responsible for any of the organization's acts of violence. This has led to considerable anxiety in the minds of the more conservative Iosans.

The Retribution leaders, called the Nine Voices, have seized upon the weakness they see in the Consulate Court and leveraged it to further their cause. They were willing to push Ios to civil war if need be but were nonetheless gratified that their political adversaries quickly caved in to their demands. They continue to press for support from any houses they perceive as even remotely sympathetic, pointing to the rising public support for the Retribution and its additional momentum since the news of Nyssor reached Ios. Politically, other hallytyr cannot vehemently oppose the Retribution without giving the impression they do not support preserving the elven gods. Relations between the consuls and the Nine Voices are tense and uncomfortable. There is a mood in the capital of a government being held hostage by radicals.

WINTER'S HAMMER
TALONS OF DAWN TASK FORCE

Drawn from the ranks of the Talons of Dawn, this huge task force and others fighting in support of its goals represent a bold move on the part of the Retribution. The mission of this force is nothing less than the recovery of the god Nyssor, believed held deep within Khador's interior by the Greylords Covenant. The task force aims to accomplish its objective quickly and efficiently but is prepared to conduct longer operations should they prove necessary. This goal represents the first priority of the Retribution, and there will be no compromises in terms of military assets sent to ensure its success.

Dawnlord Vyros Nyarr has personally assumed leadership of Winter's Hammer and intends to prove the strength of the Dawnguard by relying almost exclusively on his house's army for the main assault. He has hand-picked subordinate officers from among the most capable officers of his house, several closely related by blood. Ravyn, Eternal Light, is leading the special operations companies in support of Vyros' forces, using her mage hunters to ensure the strike proceeds as planned. Vyros has eschewed houseguard for the initial strike, reserving that honor for the Dawnguard.

Vyros has made plans, however, for houseguard companies to aid in covering the force's return to secure territory once the mission has been executed. He intends to make use of a variety of feints and ambushes during the retreat out of Khador to hamper pursuit. As the senior mage hunter warcaster, Ravyn is responsible for organizing these efforts as well as coordinating strike forces during the assault phase. The mission is of such high importance that other task forces from Scyrah's Blade will be involved in diversionary attacks inside occupied Llael that should attract Khadoran forces and divert patrols.

While the operation will rely heavily on the Dawnguard, with a moderate wing of heavy cavalry support, the core of the force is its myrmidons. Vyros' soldiers have been drilling for months using a regimen created specifically to prepare them for Khadoran tactics. The operation's secondary priority is to exact a heavy toll on the Greylords Covenant without compromising the recovery of Nyssor's frozen vault.

The Winter's Hammer task force contains a van and special operations segment drawn from the Talons of Dawn strike army.

Van Leadership
Dawnlord Vyros Nyarr, warcaster

Van Composition
1,050 Dawnguard Invictors Assault Infantry
750 Dawnguard Sentinels Heavy Infantry
200 Dawnguard Destors Heavy Cavalry
150 House Shyeel Battle Mages
20 Ghost Snipers

Warjack Support
20 Heavy, 30 Light

Special Operations Leadership
Ravyn, warcaster
Eiryss, Angel of the Retribution

Special Operations Composition
200 Mage Hunters
(including various specialties)
80 Stormfall Archers

Warjack Support
2 Heavy, 5 Light

HOUSES NYARR AND SHYEEL

Despite lingering tensions, those suggesting violently quashing the Retribution have been overruled. Such a task would be difficult and bloody at best. Though the Homeguard Coalition outnumbers the Retribution, the extremists' numbers are deceptive. Iosan military experts agree the Retribution's forces are disproportionately powerful, due primarily to the involvement of House Shyeel and House Nyarr who bring with them a vast armory of myrmidons and other arcanik weapons in addition to the Dawnguard.

Houses Nyarr and Shyeel have for years made little effort to hide their quiet support of the Retribution. Minor sympathies for Ios' fringe religious sects are not uncommon in political circles—many high-ranking nobles have such leanings. Most houses would draw the line, however, at agreeing to an open and full alliance with the Retribution, which is exactly what Houses Nyarr and Shyeel have recently done. They have even gone so far as to take the unprecedented step of allocating the majority of their military assets to Retribution service.

The truth is that these two hallytyr have been more tightly linked to the Retribution than their peers ever realized. For decades they have secretly provided both financial and military assistance to the organization. These houses decided long ago that true change in Ios would require extreme measures.

As the political creatures they are, the respective leaders of these houses have kept their motives to themselves. These men are not given to zealotry or religious fervor; it is generally accepted that House Nyarr and House Shyeel back the Retribution for pragmatic rather than religious reasons. It is not that their leaders are thought to dismiss Scyrah's condition or ignore the gravity of the status of the vanished gods, but pursuing such lofty mysteries is clearly not their primary motive for pushing the Retribution agenda.

Those who succeed in leading the cause of salvation will reap great rewards. The political clout brought by the unquestioning support of the people could facilitate the transformation of Iosan society and even the dissolution of the Consulate Court. This is a gamble to which House Nyarr and House Shyeel have committed all their considerable resources. Should the Retribution cause continue to spread among the population, the other hallytyr may feel forced to follow their example or be left powerless in the expected new order.

RETRIBUTION HIERARCHY

Growing beyond a loose association of mage hunters has required massive shifts in the Retribution's organization and hierarchy. The organization is still undergoing these fluctuations. House Nyarr has taken the initiative to assume

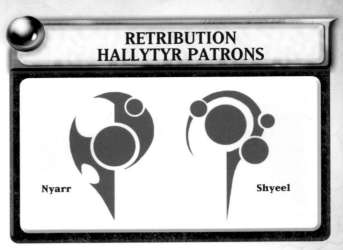

RETRIBUTION HALLYTYR PATRONS

Nyarr

Shyeel

operational control of the Retribution's military on every level. While the old guard among the mage hunters appreciates such military expertise, reliance on strict discipline and chain of command is not always immediately embraced. The Retribution is led by the Nine Voices who order its army divisions. These divisions are in turn led by the top ranking Dawnguard officers, each assisted by equivalently ranked veteran mage hunters. Dawnguard officers direct the actions of similarly ranked houseguard officers, and the chain of command descends from there to lesser officers and junior mage hunters.

RETRIBUTION OPERATIONAL REGIONS

The Retribution has divided western Immoren into a variety of operational regions where Retribution cells establish a variety of safe houses and bases. Most of these bases are small and isolated, either hidden in the wilderness or concealed in cities among those few exiled Iosans living alongside humanity.

The scale and resources of the bases vary considerably, but most are kept small to avoid detection. The Retribution has had to take particular care in placing these sites to escape discovery by area inhabitants such as blackclads or various trollkin kriels. Proximity has led to violent conflict on occasion, and the Retribution has had to erase a number of remote trollkin villages and blackclad stone circles to protect their secrets.

The largest Retribution bases outside Ios include an armory secreted in the forest northwest of Caspia; a cave complex off a sheltered cove northwest of Ceryl; an underground bunker northeast of Shattered Shield Lake, across the lake from Korsk; and a hidden observation garrison in the Llaelese mountains between Rynyr and Laedry. Dozens of other safe houses, stashes, and secured mustering points pepper western Immoren, any of which might be expanded in the years ahead as the Retribution escalates its operations. Efforts are underway to prepare many of these bases to house and service battle-ready myrmidons.

The partnership between the veteran mage hunters and Dawnguard officers is a strained one, with tensions on both sides. Dawnguard officers have assumed positions of authority at every level in the chain of command. In turn, the Nine Voices insist ranking mage hunters be present to "advise" their Dawnguard counterparts, creating leadership pairings. For example, Dawnlord Vyros Nyarr is the most proactive and prominent military leader of his house and generally assumes the mantle of overall military commander. His counterpart Ravyn, called "the Eternal Light," is the highest-ranking mage hunter commander and warcaster. The two enjoy roughly comparable statuses within the Retribution, but their areas of oversight differ.

Resentment is common on both sides and can interfere with operations if left unchecked. Mage hunters do not appreciate the regimented and inflexible military style of the Dawnguard and dislike having orders barked at them. In turn, the Dawnguard consider mage hunters to be lacking in proper military discipline, respect, and organization. The vast differences in operational styles have not been easy to bridge and are likely to remain a point of contention as the Retribution moves forward.

LEADERS OF THE RETRIBUTION

Historically, veteran agents inside Ios coordinated the Retribution's operations abroad. They formed the Nine Voices of the Retribution as a governing council. Only the most senior Retribution agents have direct contact with any of the Nine Voices, and information about them has been shrouded in secrecy. As the Retribution has become more active this has begun to change, but most Retribution soldiers still do not have a clear or complete awareness of the identities of their highest-ranking leaders. What they do know is that once the Nine Voices decide on a course, they expect nothing less than unquestioning obedience.

While technically the Nine Voices are equal, in truth some voices are stronger than others. Four leaders in particular prioritize Retribution objectives and prepare the military to execute its goals based on gathered intelligence. The most influential is Glyssor Syviis, a leading agent of the old guard who led countless assassination and espionage missions in his prime. His deeds are legendary within the organization, and he is the one member of this council whose inclusion is widely assumed.

Espionage Liaison Kelsyr Yrryel is another respected old-guard Retribution leader. He is a toughened Iosan of venerable years who helped shape the organization into what it is today. Kelsyr served as an Iosan ambassador for over half a century, spending time in the capitals of Cygnar, Khador, Llael, and Ord. He returned to Ios permanently at the outset of the civil war when the nation severed all diplomatic contact with the human nations. During his career as ambassador his

Retribution affiliation was secret, and though he has long since abandoned such pretenses, he maintains a number of foreign contacts who know nothing of his true agenda.

Consul Caelcyr Nyarr and Consul Hyselle Shyeel were until recently the most secret members of the Nine Voices, but that changed when they openly declared their house loyalties. They are two of the Retribution's most important decision makers due to the vital nature of their respective house assets. Regular political duties prevent them from attending all meetings, but the consuls send trusted proxies when necessary

The remaining five Voices are less overtly influential, but each contributes significantly to the Retribution's success. Quaestor Nyr Voshan was once a major underworld leader in Shyrr who oversaw a lucrative smuggling operation with its own small army of vicious thugs. Now he keeps track of Retribution assets and supplies, a critical task with the onset of major military operations. Keldeacon Synvas Uithuyr is a former mage hunter whose injuries in the field forced him to retire to the Syvash Stronghold where he has become the undisputed master of induction and training. He is responsible for accelerating Retribution recruitment and also seeks to identify new warcaster talent. The ancient Jarmyr of Eyvreyn is a man whose name still causes ripples in Iosan arcane circles, a controversial master of the occult whose techniques are in disfavor by his conservative peers. No one in the organization better understands the threat posed by human magic, warcasters in particular, and he bends all his vast intellect to their destruction.

WHAT'S IN A NAME?

Every soldier in the Dawnguard is a member of House Nyarr, in oath if not by blood. Not every person included in this house uses Nyarr as a surname; only those with a direct blood tie to the original Nyarr lineage can claim that privilege. The house includes hundreds of lesser families with no direct blood ties. Over the centuries these families have been adopted into House Nyarr as they were invited to join the ranks of the Dawnguard. While these soldiers may informally speak of themselves as "brothers" or "cousins," most of them are not blood-related. Arranged marriages between these families can complicate matters even further. A similar situation exists in each of the hallytyr, such as House Shyeel, as well as the lesser noble houses. Each consists of dozens of allied families led by the direct blood inheritors of the house name and leadership.

Leading priest Oracle Relvinor Luynmyr strives to ensure the goddess Scyrah is not forgotten during deliberations. Relvinor is arguably the most fanatic and charismatic of the Nine Voices, a man of fiery rhetoric driven by absolute conviction in the righteousness of his holy cause. His clergy works to spread the organization's religious message both in political circles and among the population. His top aide, Orator Lysenne Bylvesh, was a member of the conservative Fane of Scyrah before Relvinor converted her, and she has done much to drive a wedge into her former priesthood and bring additional converts to the Retribution.

THE MAGE HUNTERS

Though the Retribution has greatly increased in size and scope, the core of the original organization remains. Its membership, the mage hunters, embody the fundamental convictions of the cause. These efficient killers have worked outside Ios for centuries, divided into clandestine cells conducting operations within the human kingdoms.

The primary purpose of these cells is to execute strikes against human wizards and warcasters. They conduct missions to gather information, to sabotage arcane research and mechanikal production facilities, and to assassinate significant human arcanists. The cells focus on undermining the most pervasive and powerful organizations of human wizards, particularly those serving military interests such as Khador's Greylords Covenant or Cygnar's Militant Order of the Arcane Tempest. They have additionally struck against private organizations like the Fraternal Order of Wizardry and the Order of the Golden Crucible. The pace and execution of these attacks is carefully calculated to avoid compromising their secrecy.

Mage hunters comprise the espionage and assassination arm of the Retribution, supported by sleeper agents throughout the Iron Kingdoms. Several mage hunters have manifested warcaster talent. Having undergone additional training to refine these skills, they serve as the deadliest of the Retribution's strike leaders. These warcasters are not permanently tied to any specific task force. Instead they move frequently between operational regions as ordered by the Nine Voices.

Mage hunter talents at obfuscation and deception serve them well in strikes against human military targets. Their preexisting network of secret bases across western Immoren provides the Retribution with far greater mobility and reach than outsiders might expect. These resources and operatives make it possible to conduct very deep strikes within the interior of human kingdoms.

A small but fanatical priesthood encourages and actively supports the mage hunters. These priests are dedicated to a radical interpretation of Scyrah's faith that predates the Retribution. They describe the goddess as a battle-ready maiden, not the peaceful avatar of spring traditionally depicted. Human deities, they believe, worked together to strike her down alongside the other members of the Divine Court as part of some nefarious scheme to bestow arcane lore on the unworthy human species. The priesthood strives to ensure mage hunters never waver in their convictions. Their preaching encourages mage hunters to remember the imminent doom of their people—a doom only their acts can forestall.

MYRMIDON INVENTION

Though the citizens of the old Empire of Lyoss were versed in advanced arcanika, myrmidons are a relatively recent innovation. The power systems and intricate mechanical elements are based on considerably older and well-established arcane technologies, but the idea of using those techniques to create battle-ready automatons arose as a result of seeing the effective use of such machines by humanity. Elven agents observed how the colossals repulsed the Orgoth and how effective the smaller warjacks proved in later wars.

Arcanika specialist houses such as Shyeel and Vyre were confident they could replicate the warjack chassis and even greatly improve upon them. The most vital missing element was the fabrication process for a central controlling device that would enable the machines to operate semi-autonomously. While these hallytyr do not openly acknowledge the fact, fabrication of myrmidon cortexes was made possible by the theft and deconstruction of those of human warjacks. The Iosan versions were considerably redesigned and bear no resemblance to their human-made counterparts. It is likely no one in the Retribution aside from House Shyeel artificers has any idea of the role played by human cortexes in the invention of these devices. Given mage hunter attitudes toward human mechanika, this is probably for the best.

Mage hunters believe human magic is a blight on Scyrah and therefore every eliminated human wizard or sorcerer relieves the goddess' suffering a little more. They see human mechanika as similarly tainted and its proliferation a contributor to Scyrah's incapacitation. By escalating to full war the organization hopes to eradicate the affliction permanently and thereby restore the goddess to her former health. No measure is too extreme given the stakes. If the Retribution must annihilate every human warcaster, wizard, and warjack to achieve their goal, so be it. Some conduct this task coldly, simply as a pragmatic necessity, while others enjoy their bloody work and nurse a deep and abiding hatred of humanity.

Finding and training skilled mage hunters remains as difficult as it is essential. Most of the recent upswing in Retribution membership has been among the houseguard soldiery, not the mage hunters. It takes a special combination of zeal, ruthlessness, and raw combat prowess to become a mage hunter. Senior agents are always looking for good prospects to send to the Syvash Stronghold to be transformed into efficient stalkers and hunters of mankind. Those who survive the early difficult years may be asked to return for additional specialized training according to their individual aptitudes. A broad range of specialties reinforces the mage hunter ranks, including wilderness trackers, expert bladesmen, marksmen, mechanikal disruptors, and experts of intrusion and espionage.

At the top of their field are the living legends: mage hunters like Eiryss, the most renowned mage hunter of Ios, or Garryth, Blade of Retribution. All junior mage hunters aspire to reach such heights, and they are more than willing to climb a mountain of human corpses to do it.

THE DAWNGUARD AND THE HOUSEGUARD

Commanded by House Nyarr, the Dawnguard is a martial order with roots stretching back to the ancient Lyoss Empire. It has evolved into a highly efficient and self-contained army capable of conducting extensive military operations with little to no external support. The Dawnguard fields a versatile mix of infantry and cavalry as well as more focused specialists, and its soldiers are armed with the most advanced Iosan weapons and armor. Dawnguard are implacable warriors, drilled to coordinate their actions and conditioned to be absolutely loyal to House Nyarr. They serve the Retribution because their house leaders have ordered them to do so, not from any personal commitment to the cause.

The Dawnguard is divided into three branches: the Sentinels, the Invictors, and the Destors. The Sentinels and Invictors together comprise the elite infantry of the Retribution military. The Destors are the heavy cavalry of the force.

Officer commissions in the Dawnguard are based on a combination of blood ties and service performance. Many top-ranking officers in the Dawnguard are also nobles of House Nyarr, including its current dawnlords, though in the order's history there have been several examples of officers from outside the noble family rising to this esteemed rank. While technically all dawnlords are equal and subordinate to Consul Caelcyr Nyarr, the warcaster Dawnlord Vyros Nyarr is deferred to as the ranking field commander.

The houseguard is not nearly as cohesive or simply structured. These loose companies are populated with soldiers who either volunteered to join the Retribution or were dispatched by their houses. The houseguard makes up the rank and file line of the Retribution military and includes both commoners and noble-born soldiers.

The men and women of the houseguard may seem identical to their counterparts in the direct service of Ios, but there are significant differences in motivation and resolve. Those who serve the Homeguard Coalition have chosen the safer career, as Ios' borders have historically seen little conflict. Those who volunteered to join the Retribution have done so despite the censure of disapproving families and have chosen a path of certain peril. Many have volunteered from a strong belief in the Retribution cause, inspired by recent events and the rhetoric of Retribution recruiters and priests. Some of the lesser houses that provide houseguard companies hope to secure alliances with Nyarr and Shyeel and perhaps one day share in their fortunes.

Among the houseguard are experienced career soldiers belonging to companies that joined the Retribution at the behest of a noble to whom they have sworn loyalty. A number of middle-tier nobles agreed to help the Retribution and have sent their house soldiers to fight as a demonstration of solidarity. While such soldiers may lack the fervor of volunteer recruits, they bring years of experience. Their pragmatic approach is an appreciated balance to the zealotry of enthusiastic youth.

Houseguard provide the bulk of the Retribution's numbers, primarily halberdiers and riflemen. This is the main body of the Retribution army, and its basic role is to leverage its massed strength where such numbers are most effective. Houseguard forces are used to hold ground, occupy enemy forces, or thin enemy ranks by delivering massed fire. Engagements unfold with houseguard forces tying up the enemy while mage hunters advance past the lines to strike at the head, such as a commanding warcaster. In other engagements the line is tasked to pin the enemy in place while Dawnguard maneuver to crush them from a different angle of attack.

Though houseguard soldiers do not receive the same acclaim as Dawnguard or mage hunters, they can expect to endure heavy casualties during massed battle. The stark fact of their regular sacrifices and bravery garners them deep respect from the more specialized elements of the Retribution military. In time, specific houseguard companies will distinguish themselves and earn reputations for valor in battle. Others may be destroyed to the last man and be forgotten by all but their mourning kinsmen. Such is life in the line.

ARMY DIVISIONS AND TASK FORCES

The Retribution currently has partitioned its major military assets into three army divisions. Two of the divisions serve as standing strike armies. These larger armies include the bulk of the Dawnguard and houseguard companies, along with substantial mage hunter support. Mage hunters dominate the third division, using their favored organization and methods of operation with its heavy use of covert operations and small surgical strikes.

The primary strike army, referred to as the "Talons of Dawn," receives first priority of equipment and personnel. Led by Dawnlord Vyros Nyarr himself, this standing army represents the greatest concentration of Retribution military might and therefore tackles the highest priority objectives. It was this army, for instance, that was dispatched into Khador to recover the god Nyssor.

The secondary strike army, called "Scyrah's Blade," stands ready to support the primary army or to attack other priority targets simultaneously. Dawnlord Cyrsyll Nyarr commands this division; she is a respected senior member of her house and a blood cousin of Dawnlord Vyros. This force has several priorities but has been given the long-term task of expanding Ios' borders while laying the foundation for strikes abroad.

The enigmatic third division is called the "Unseen Spear" and is composed of the Retribution's Ancillary Strike Teams. This force exists to allow the Retribution to conduct smaller strikes and operations unrelated to the actions of the main armies, and its members have been specifically chosen for their adaptability and initiative. Dawnguard Issyr Rylavos supervises the Unseen Spear, but the division sometimes receives priority orders directly from the Nine Voices. The senior Retribution warcaster commanding this army is Kaelyssa, known as "Night's Whisper." She is a strike team leader with an exemplary performance record and proven loyalty to the Retribution.

Unseen Spear teams may be sent deep into enemy territory, going where columns of soldiers could not. They work closely with Retribution field agents in these operational regions and make use of hidden bunkers, weapons stashes, and armories. They are often out of contact with leadership for extended periods of time and are afforded significant leeway in executing their orders. The lack of direct oversight for these groups has been a point of contention between Dawnguard and mage hunter leaders. Senior Issyr Rylavos can rarely claim to know precisely what the teams under his command are doing.

The three army divisions defining the military hierarchy of the Retribution are rarely sent to war in their entirety. Lacking sufficient numbers and support for engagements of such magnitude, the Retribution instead commits its military in smaller operational groups, known as task forces, for specific operations. Each task force typically draws from the elements of a single army. When task forces from two or more armies take part in the same operation, the ranking officer pair takes field command.

Task force composition varies greatly, as each draws from the full complement of an army according to its operational requirements. Some operations involve a single strike to eliminate a key target while others are intricate or open-ended missions over an extended period. Efforts to rescue Nyssor from Khador, for example, comprise an extremely complex series of coordinated operations by multiple task forces. A task force may include personnel from the Dawnguard, mage hunters, houseguard, battle mages, myrmidons, and a variety of support and specialist groups. This system affords the Retribution considerable operational flexibility and makes it an unpredictable enemy on the battlefield.

Mage hunters are quite comfortable within the framework of these unconventional military practices, but the Dawnguard and houseguard forces still struggle to accept the methodology fully. The Dawnguard ranks have adopted the Retribution's flexible doctrine with little grumbling, but its upper echelons remain protective of their chain of command. Most ranking Dawnguard officers insist they must vet any order concerning the disposition of units under their command even when it comes through the most senior of mage hunter agents. In turn, the mage hunters jealously guard their operational freedom against Dawnguard officers who seek a complete understanding of the actions of their subordinate units. Cooperation is not always easy. There is considerable tension in any mixed force, yet when battle ensues, each side knows its place and functions even as the two continue to learn to work together toward shared objectives.

UNUSUAL ALLIES

The Retribution has attracted assistance from several unexpected quarters. Given the weight of public sentiment it appears to be too late to forestall the organization's violent policies. Groups opposing them have had to face this reality, and some have decided to try subtler means to steer the radicals from a path they fear will culminate in Ios' destruction.

The Fane of Scyrah is the most influential group that has dispatched agents to "observe and advise" the Retribution. The conservative fane knows it has lost considerable clout in the present political arena, as the common people see its members as indolent and timid. Its reputation is worsened by the knowledge that its priests have had the privilege of the greatest direct contact with the ailing goddess and yet have done little to aid her. The fane knows it must understand the Retribution if it is to come to grips with the growing unrest of the people.

The differences between the Fane of Scyrah and the Retribution's more extreme religious views seem irreconcilable. In particular, the fane believes any spiritual magic invoked by their priests drains Scyrah. This has been the primary reason for their unwillingness to commit to extreme action: traditional priests believe Retribution clergy are causing irreversible harm to the goddess. The Retribution clergy, though, believe they have established ways to invoke this sort of power without doing harm to the goddess. Furthermore, they insist that any energy expended by the priesthood is insignificant compared to the egregious damage dealt to Scyrah every day by thousands of human arcanists. When it comes to waging war against the enemies of the goddess, they maintain they must use every weapon at their disposal.

BARBED THORN
SCYRAH'S BLADE TASK FORCE

The task force called "Barbed Thorn," led by Adeptis Rahn, has been sent by Scyrah's Blade in support of Vyros Nyarr's main assault. Barbed Thorn's mission is to disrupt Khadoran patrols along a heavily traveled corridor in western Llael, enabling Winter's Hammer to slip into the Khadoran interior. Rahn is joined by Garryth, Blade of Retribution, and the mage hunter strike forces under his command. Other task forces will be engaged with related troop movements and diversionary attacks inside occupied Llael and elsewhere, but this operation is the most crucial.

Adeptis Rahn plans to utilize the houseguard to provoke several sizable Khadoran garrisons near Laedry and bait them into pursuit into the northern mountains. By occupying secure ground and taking advantage of elevation, cover, and choke points, the adeptis is confident he can keep his forces safe indefinitely even if Khador mounts a sizable pursuit force. The more enemy attention and reinforcements hurled in their direction, the better. These strikes are being coordinated with the movements of Dawnlord Vyros and his heavy assault force, which will bypass this region to continue west. Similar efforts will be undertaken when the dawnlord retreats, hopefully with Nyssor safely in his protection.

Retribution leaders expect this operation to endure heavy casualties, most of which will be suffered by the houseguard companies. After they have succeeded in their own tasks, elements of Scyrah's Blade and the Unseen Spear will make every effort to extricate the survivors. Those remnants will be reincorporated into the main army and then tasked with expanding a region of control near Ios' southern border.

Leadership
Adeptis Rahn Shyeel, warcaster
Garryth, Blade of Retribution, warcaster

Composition
1,200 Houseguard Halberdiers Infantry
2,500 Houseguard Riflemen Infantry
150 Dawnguard Invictors
70 Dawnguard Sentinels
80 Mage Hunters
60 Stormfall Archers
50 House Shyeel Battle Mages
20 Ghost Snipers

Warjack Support
4 Heavy, 12 Light

Despite this stance, a thread of sympathy for the Retribution cause persists within the Fane of Scyrah priesthood that reaches even to the top ranks. Auricant Avross Larisar and Glyssor Syviis periodically meet in secret to discuss the plight of the goddess. Such secret supporters loathe the Retribution's methods even while envying the sect's decisiveness. In addition, several members of the Fane Knights have decided to accompany the Retribution armies into foreign lands. Having sworn fealty to Scyrah, these knights seek to test Retribution claims that war against human magic is their best hope to restore her.

In addition to the Fane of Scyrah, a variety of less prominent groups have also taken notice of the Retribution's popularity. These include the Seekers, a more moderate sect. This group has reluctantly offered its counsel, perhaps hoping to encourage the Retribution to focus on the search for a solution to Scyrah's dilemma rather than persisting in widespread systematic violence. The arcanists of these two sects cooperate as necessary, but always with an undercurrent of suspicion, dislike, and distrust.

Retribution leaders are not blind to the subversive goals of their supposed allies and know some have joined only to spy on their activities. Nonetheless, so long as they prove useful the Retribution is content to let such individuals remain. It is to their advantage to be inclusive in their membership, thereby spreading their message as far as possible. Given time and the proper persuasion, some of the spies might even become true converts to the cause.

RETRIBUTION WARCASTERS AND MYRMIDONS

Having only recently devoted their energy to open war, the Retribution does not have the same experience identifying and training warcasters as the human armies. Fortunately House Shyeel and House Nyarr have effective systems in place for training such individuals. The techniques they employ have been passed to the Syvash Stronghold, the Retribution's main training base in Iryss. The Retribution considers it a top priority to expand its warcaster assets as quickly as possible.

The exact authority of warcasters is less clearly defined in the Retribution than in human armies. A warcaster may not always have complete control over a given force although in practice they are usually afforded operational oversight. The importance of a warcaster's battle magic and control of precious myrmidons means they always have a central role in any given battle. The most common source of tension comes from Dawnguard officers who may be slow to answer the commands of mage hunter warcasters. If the allocation of task forces assigns the same soldiers to fight together in several battles such interpersonal issues tend to be resolved, one way or another.

This is never a problem with those warcasters who occupy clear positions of authority. Dawnguard Vyros Nyarr and Adeptis Rahn Shyeel are widely recognized battle leaders of their houses. Additionally, the Nine Voices have made it clear that Ravyn, the Eternal Light, speaks with the full authority of the ruling council. The proper chain of command becomes less clear when applied to strike leaders like Garryth, the Blade

THE SOULLESS

One of the most controversial aspects of the Retribution is its use of soulless warriors. For centuries the organization has accepted soulless children from parents who could not bear the thought of having them killed at birth. This remains a taboo topic in Ios—and another area where the Retribution is at odds with the Fane of Scyrah.

The Retribution insists they are doing the soulless a service by allowing them to contribute to the holy cause. Mage hunters know they make exemplary assassins when trained properly. While soulless lack empathy and most emotions, they follow orders without hesitation. They suffer none of the moral qualms of normal soldiers and can become efficient killers. A special branch of the Syvash Stronghold handles their upbringing and training, indoctrinating them with a special code of behavior intended to substitute for a missing conscience.

The Retribution has discovered supernatural side effects of employing soulless. These individuals have an unusual impact on magic in their vicinity, which can be used as both a weapon and a defense. The Retribution has only an imperfect understanding of these manifestations and is working to be able to manipulate them more effectively. For the time being, it is not uncommon that soulless accompany units assigned to important tasks in order to help divert hostile magic by sacrificing themselves.

Soulless work most closely with mage hunters, so the majority of rank-and-file soldiers have limited experience with them. Soulless are not afforded the same stature as regular mage hunters or other soldiers. Because they have no ambition, family obligation, or leadership ability, they are also not afforded normal ranks or honors. They are treated as expendable weapons rather than as individuals and rarely interact with others outside of what is required during combat. Even the names they are given are short and simple with no connections to family or Iosan history. Senior mage hunters are pragmatic regarding the soulless, knowing that if they had not been given over to fight for the cause each of them would have been killed at birth. Every day they live to fight for the Retribution is considered a mercy and a gift.

of Retribution, or Kaelyssa, Night's Whisper. These warcasters can expect obedience from mage hunter forces but rarely lead large composite task forces.

In the past, myrmidons were rarely utilized in attacks on human targets since their capture or discovery would have undermined the covert nature of their missions. There have been several notable exceptions where Retribution warcasters unleashed their power to erase a human arcane workshop or lodge completely. The destruction left by these attacks was blamed on other causes—rival human governments or freak supernatural occurrences, for example—and no one except possibly the victims knew they were the targets of carefully orchestrated Iosan assaults.

The Retribution has been so successful with these measures that most humans are unaware of myrmidons' very existence, let alone their strengths and weaknesses. This will change as Retribution actions abroad become more common, but for now widespread ignorance of Retribution capabilities provides a significant edge in battle.

Myrmidons are different from human and Rhulic warjacks in several significant respects, which has a profound impact on how they are maintained, supplied, and deployed. Handling these tasks is a priority for the support segment of the Retribution military. The Retribution must be able to cross great distances quickly and covertly, obliterate their targets, and return to Ios rapidly. Because of the remote nature of these missions, Retribution task forces cannot let themselves be pinned down by human armies. Their strategy is one of overwhelming attack followed by swift withdrawal.

Due to their arcanik power sources, myrmidons are greatly liberated from the limitations of conventional supply lines, which affords them unparalleled mobility. Damaged myrmidons still require occasional replacement parts and Retribution soldiers still require food and ammunition, so supply lines are not altogether unimportant. Nonetheless, freedom from the need for constant resupply of fuel gives myrmidons greater speed and range of redeployment compared to their steam-powered counterparts in other armies. Furthermore, Retribution forces stockpile other needed supplies in operational regions when possible to avoid the complications of continually shipping gear across long distances.

Though they draw their own power from their environs, myrmidons cannot run indefinitely at battle capacity. Myrmidons operating at peak capacity will deplete their energy cells after a few hours and require time to recharge by sitting idle. This places an even higher importance on Retribution planning and logistics. In an ideal Retribution engagement, the battle is over long before energy cells are depleted. If a Retribution battlegroup is attacked

MYRMIDON POWER SOURCE

One of the fundamental differences between human or Rhulic mechanika and Iosan arcanika relates to power source. Unlike other types of warjacks, myrmidons do not utilize a fuel-fed steam boiler as an external combustion engine. They rely instead on a more arcane and self-sustaining power plant that requires neither the burning of coal or other fuel nor periodic water resupply. Instead of creating energy from an exothermic reaction, it uses an arcane condenser to siphon latent energy from the surroundings, augmented and regulated by subtle geomantic and celestial alignments. After being condensed, power is accumulated into storage cells. Energy can subsequently be released to drive motors powering a myrmidon's limbs or diverted into a myrmidon's energy field. This system bears superficial similarity to the storm chambers developed by Cygnar, but the underlying functionality is radically different.

To human mechanikal understanding it appears as if these engines create power from nothing, but the truth is both less miraculous and considerably more complicated. It is technically possible to deprive a myrmidon of power by insulating it entirely from its surroundings, but in practice this rarely happens.

The arcane power source allows several related technologies, including the use of strong protective fields that can deflect incoming attacks as well as power energy-based ranged weapons. Accordingly most myrmidons do not require ammunition but are also unable to fire when these systems are severely damaged.

unexpectedly it may be caught with drained and useless myrmidons. It is vital to keep this potential weakness secret as long as possible, lest the enemies of the Retribution find a way to exploit it.

Unlike their human enemies, Retribution forces do not need to haul their 'jacks into position on trains or wagons. The trickle of power from the arcane condenser is sufficient to allow myrmidons continuous movement at a moderate pace. While on the march, a myrmidon's power field is typically kept inactive and its arms and weapons systems are unpowered. Switching to full battle readiness can take several minutes as the flow of energy is increased and reallocated. Myrmidons ambushed in this state can easily be destroyed before they retaliate. This situation is exacerbated if the myrmidons have been pushed to travel more rapidly, which gradually drains energy reserves even outside of battle.

The established procedure for battlegroups on the move is to march as quickly as possible from one point of safety to another, avoiding conflict while in transit. At each safe point myrmidons are kept idle long enough to recharge before the force pushes on to a mustering point near the operational objective. Ideally, myrmidons become fully charged before committing to battle.

The importance of planning and reconnaissance for the Retribution cannot be overstated. Arriving at a remote location without drawing enemy attention can be difficult for even a modestly sized task force. Strategically placed supply caches and accurate information on the locations of enemy patrols and garrisons are vital. When these elements combine correctly and the Retribution can strike on their terms, they have unparalleled strength. When they are caught by surprise or forced into a protracted engagement, on the other hand, the weaknesses of their systems make them far more vulnerable.

Myrmidons are a limited and precious resource, and sometimes a warcaster must make do with what is available. Requests by warcasters for additional myrmidon support within an army are fulfilled based on ever-changing priorities. All else being equal, warcasters attached to the Talons of Dawn receive their first pick of myrmidons, leaving the remainder first to Scyrah's Blade and then to the Unseen Spear. Myrmidon allocations can be tricky; such decisions are the province of House Shyeel, which manufactures and maintains the 'jacks. This house sometimes exercises its political clout through these allocations. For example, Adeptis Rahn Shyeel can expect to receive any myrmidons he requests regardless of where he is stationed, even in preference over Dawnlord Vyros. Every officer and coordinator in the Retribution knows the importance of treating members of House Shyeel with due respect if they wish to keep their myrmidons in proper fighting trim.

RETRIBUTION RULES

THEME FORCES

Theme Forces are themed armies for specific warcasters. A Theme Force can include only one warcaster. If you are playing a game with two or more warcasters in each army, you cannot use these rules.

Theme Forces are broken into tiers. Each tier has a set of requirements that restricts your army composition. If your army meets the requirements of a tier, you gain the benefits

listed. These benefits are cumulative: you gain the benefits of every tier for which your army meets the requirements.

If a Theme Force can include a given unit, you can add any attachments to that unit that are available to it.

The following Theme Forces are available to Retribution warcasters.

ADEPTIS RAHN
CHARGE OF THE BATTLE MAGES

TIER 1

Requirements: Adeptis Rahn is the warcaster. In addition, the army includes only models/units that are non-character Retribution warjacks, Houseguard units, House Shyeel Battle Mage units, Arcanist solos, or House Shyeel Battle Mage Magister solos.

Benefit: House Shyeel Battle Mage units in the army become FA U. Additionally, the FA of House Shyeel Magister solos in the army increases by +1 for each Battle Mage unit included.

TIER 2

Requirements: In addition to meeting all the requirements listed for Tier 1, the army includes two or more heavy warjacks.

Benefit: Add one Arcanist solo to the army free of cost. This model does not count toward FA restrictions.

TIER 3

Requirements: In addition to meeting all the requirements listed for Tier 2, the army includes three or more House Shyeel Magister solos.

Benefit: House Shyeel Battle Mage units and House Shyeel Battle Mage Magister solos in the army gain Advance Move. Models with Advance Move can make a full advance after both players have deployed but before the first player's first turn.

TIER 4

Requirements: In addition to meeting all the requirements listed for Tier 3, the army includes four or more House Shyeel Battle Mage units.

Benefit: Friendly models/units can begin the game affected by Rahn's upkeep spells. These spells and their targets must be declared before either player sets up models. Rahn does not pay focus to upkeep these spells during your first turn.

DAWNLORD VYROS
LEGIONS OF THE DAWN

TIER 1

Requirements: Dawnlord Vyros is the warcaster. In addition, the army includes only models/units that are non-character Retribution warjacks, Dawnguard units, Stormfall Archer units, Arcanist solos, or Dawnguard solos.

Benefit: Dawnguard Invictor and Dawnguard Sentinel units in the army become FA U. Additionally, the FA of Dawnguard Scyir solos in the army increases by +1 for each Dawnguard Sentinel or Dawnguard Invictor unit included.

TIER 2

Requirements: In addition to meeting all the requirements listed for Tier 1, the army includes two or more Dawnguard Sentinel units.

Benefit: Add a unit attachment to one Dawnguard Sentinel unit in the army free of cost. This unit attachment ignores FA restrictions.

TIER 3

Requirements: In addition to meeting all the requirements listed for Tier 2, the army includes one Dawnguard Destor unit *and* one or more Dawnguard Destor Thane solos.

Benefit: You gain +1 on your starting game roll.

TIER 4

Requirements: In addition to meeting all the requirements listed for Tier 3, Vyros' battlegroup includes two or more heavy warjacks.

Benefit: Your deployment is extended 2″ forward.

KAELYSSA, NIGHT'S WHISPER
SHADOWS OF RETRIBUTION

TIER 1

Requirements: Kaelyssa, Night's Whisper, is the warcaster. In addition, the army includes only models/units that are non-character Retribution warjacks, Mage Hunter units, Arcanist solos, Ghost Sniper solos, or Mage Hunter solos.

Benefit: Mage Hunter Strike Force units in the army become FA U.

TIER 2

Requirements: In addition to meeting all the requirements listed for Tier 1, the army also includes two or more Mage Hunter Strike Force units.

Benefit: Add a unit attachment to one Mage Hunter Strike Force unit in the army free of cost. This unit attachment does not count toward FA restrictions.

TIER 3

Requirements: In addition to meeting all the requirements listed for Tier 2, the army includes four or more Mage Hunter solos.

Benefit: You can redeploy any one Mage Hunter model/unit after both players have deployed but before the first player's first turn. The redeployed models must be placed on the table in a location they could have been deployed initially.

TIER 4

Requirements: In addition to meeting all the requirements listed for Tier 3, Kaelyssa's battlegroup includes three or more warjacks.

Benefit: Your deployment is extended 2″ forward.

GARRYTH, BLADE OF RETRIBUTION
ASSASSINS

TIER 1

Requirements: Garryth, Blade of Retribution, is the warcaster. In addition, the army includes only models/units that are non-character Retribution warjacks, Mage Hunter units, Mage Hunter Assassin solos, or Nayl.

Benefit: Mage Hunter Strike Force units in the army become FA U. Additionally, the FA of Mage Hunter Assassin solos in this army increases by +1 for each Mage Hunter Strike Force unit included.

TIER 2

Requirements: In addition to meeting all the requirements listed for Tier 1, the army also includes three or more Mage Hunter Assassin solos.

Benefit: You gain +1 on your starting game roll.

TIER 3

Requirements: In addition to meeting all the requirements listed for Tier 2, the army also includes three Mage Hunter Strike Force units each with a Soulless Escort weapon attachment.

Benefit: Add Nayl to the army free of cost.

TIER 4

Requirements: In addition to meeting all the requirements listed for Tier 3, Garryth's battlegroup includes only light warjacks.

Benefit: Models in Garryth's battlegroup gain Advance Deployment.

RAVYN, ETERNAL LIGHT
WILL OF THE NINE VOICES

TIER 1

Requirements: Ravyn, Eternal Light, is the warcaster. In addition, the army includes only models/units that are non-character Retribution warjacks, Dawnguard Invictor units, Mage Hunter units, Stormfall Archer units, Mage Hunter solos, or the Fane Knight Skyreth Issyen.

Benefit: Mage Hunter Strike Force units and Mage Hunter Strike Force unit attachments in the army become FA U.

TIER 2

Requirements: In addition to meeting all the requirements listed for Tier 1, the army also includes three or more Mage Hunter Strike Force units.

Benefit: Add one Mage Hunter solo to the army free of cost. This model is subject to FA restrictions.

TIER 3

Requirements: In addition to meeting all the requirements listed for Tier 2, the army includes Fane Knight Skyreth Issyen *and* Narn.

Benefit: You gain +1 on your starting game roll.

TIER 4

Requirements: In addition to meeting all the requirements listed for Tier 3, Ravyn's battlegroup includes two or more Phoenix warjacks.

Benefit: Each warjack in Ravyn's battlegroup is automatically allocated 1 focus point at the start of your first Control Phase. This focus is in addition to any points Ravyn allocates.

MYRMIDONS

Myrmidons are warjacks. In addition to the standard warjack rules (see *WARMACHINE: Prime Mk II*, "Warjacks") myrmidons have the following rule:

MYRMIDON ARCANTRIK FIELD

Myrmidons have two damage tracks: a set of boxes representing their force fields and another representing their damage grids. Mark the field boxes before marking the damage grids. The G boxes of a myrmidon's damage grid represent its Field Generator.

Once per turn during its activation, a myrmidon can spend 1 focus point to remove d3 damage points from its field damage track unless its Field Generator is crippled.

GARRYTH, BLADE OF RETRIBUTION
RETRIBUTION WARCASTER

By my blades I promise our enemies will soon have ample company in the afterlife. —Garryth, Blade of Retribution

GARRYTH						
SPD	STR	MAT	RAT	DEF	ARM	CMD
7	6	8	6	16	14	8

PISTOLS				
x2	RNG	ROF	AOE	POW
	12	1	–	12

BLADES		
x2	POW	P+S
	5	11

FOCUS	6
DAMAGE	16
FIELD ALLOWANCE	C
WARJACK POINTS	+5
SMALL BASE	

FEAT: VORTEX LOCK

Though it takes a great toll on his mind and body, Garryth can unleash a dark vortex of disruptive power that siphons and absorbs all arcane power in his surroundings. It leaves the air itself depleted, barren, and incapable of sustaining the magic of his enemies. While they despair, the Blade of Retribution strikes.

For one round, while in Garryth's control area enemy models cannot cast spells, channel spells, spend focus points, or be moved by place effects.

GARRYTH

🜂 Pathfinder

🜁 Stealth

Arcane Assassin – When making attacks, ignore focus points overboosting the target's Power Field and spell effects adding to its ARM or DEF.

Parry – This model cannot be targeted by free strikes.

PISTOLS

🜂 Magical Weapon

BLADES

🜂 Magical Weapon

🜁 Weapon Master

Grievous Wounds – When a model is hit by this weapon, for one round it loses Tough, cannot heal or be healed, and cannot transfer damage.

SPELLS	COST	RNG	AOE	POW	UP	OFF
DEATH SENTENCE	2	8	–	–	YES	YES

When a friendly Faction model misses target enemy model/unit with an attack, it can reroll the attack roll. Each attack roll can be rerolled only once as a result of Death Sentence.

GALLOWS	3	10	–	13	NO	YES

When an enemy model is hit by this attack, it can be pushed d6" directly toward Gallows' point of origin.

MIRAGE	3	6	–	–	YES	NO

Target friendly Faction model/unit gains Apparition. During your Control Phase, place models with Apparition anywhere completely within 2" of their current locations. If Mirage affects a unit, only models in formation can be placed.

PSYCHIC VAMPIRE	3	SELF	CTRL	–	YES	NO

When an enemy model casts a spell or uses an animus while in this model's control area, the enemy model suffers 1 damage point and this model heals 1 damage point.

TACTICAL TIPS

Gallows – This means the model is moved before it suffers damage.

Mirage – Remember that troopers must be placed in formation.

Even among mage hunters Garryth is considered a fanatic. He feels no shame and offers no apology for his talent for cold-blooded murder. He is long past caring about the lives he ends, for each kill serves a purpose. He sweeps across the battlefield like a living storm, letting the death reaped by his pistols and their razor-sharp blades serve as his prayers to the stricken goddess. No warcaster in Ios has his length of experience fighting mankind, and this affords him an almost terrifying mystique.

Garryth was discovered and recruited from the criminal underworld of Shyrr as a natural killer who could strike without regret, hesitation, or remorse. He adapted quickly to mage hunter methods. In an attempt to harness his unique potential, his mentors introduced him to an ancient Lyossan fighting style once practiced by an obscure cult of suicidal warrior-monks sworn to the god Ossyris. These monks marched to war alongside regular soldiers and stalked enemy commanders from the shadows when battle began, ending them one by one. Garryth sees his role in the Retribution in a similar light. Others fight battles—Garryth ends them.

Although capable of leading others, the Blade of Retribution prefers his own company. Beneath his brooding countenance is a mind never at rest, torn between disciplined dedication to the mission at hand and a wild desire to unleash his hatred on humanity. At times he indulges this darker nature, and in these moments he becomes an unstoppable fiend capable of acts even his allies would judge to be extreme. That he is pious is without question, but his conception of the goddess is radical even among his brethren: in his mind Scyrah is a wounded warrior-maiden with blazing eyes who stokes the anger in his heart with demands to slake her unquenchable thirst for revenge.

Unlike most warcasters currently enlisted by the Retribution, Garryth has spent little time in Ios over the last few decades. He has lived constantly in the field, becoming fluent in the languages and methods of his nation's enemies. He is one of the few Retribution warcasters with extensive experience pitting myrmidons against human adversaries; his only true peers in this are active veterans like Narn and Eiryss. To these displaced assassins Ios is an abstract dream, not a home. They seek solace only in their killing, a task with no remembered beginning or conceivable end.

Garryth finds this work endlessly gratifying. He has long anticipated the day the shackles would be removed and he would be given the liberty to kill without restraint.

Do not mistake irreverence for a lack of faith. She proves her commitment by actions, not words. —Ravyn, the Eternal Light

KAELYSSA

SPD	STR	MAT	RAT	DEF	ARM	CMD
6	6	6	7	16	14	8

RUNEBOLT CANNON

RNG	ROF	AOE	POW
12	3	–	10

VENGEANCE

POW	P+S
6	12

FOCUS	7
DAMAGE	16
FIELD ALLOWANCE	C
WARJACK POINTS	+7
SMALL BASE	

FEAT: THE VANISHING

With a single whispered word, Kaelyssa brings the curtain of night down around her. It drapes her allies in enveloping shadows and hides them from enemy eyes.

For one round, while in Kaelyssa's control area friendly Faction models gain Stealth and cannot be charged.

KAELYSSA

🌑 **Pathfinder**

True Sight – This model ignores concealment, Camouflage, and Stealth.

Witch Hound – If a model in this model's battlegroup in its control area is hit by an enemy magic attack, immediately after the attack is resolved one model in this model's battlegroup in its control area can make a full advance and make one normal attack.

RUNEBOLT CANNON

💫 **Magical Weapon**

Energy Siphon – When this attack hits an enemy model with 1 or more focus or fury points on it, that model loses 1 focus or fury point and this model gains 1 focus point.

VENGEANCE

💫 **Magical Weapon**

Energy Siphon – When this attack hits an enemy model with 1 or more focus or fury points on it, that model loses 1 focus or fury point and this model gains 1 focus point.

SPELLS	COST	RNG	AOE	POW	UP	OFF
ARCANTRIK BOLT	2	10	–	12	NO	YES
A warjack damaged by this attack becomes stationary for one round.						
ARCANE RECKONING	3	6	–	–	YES	NO
Target friendly Faction model/unit gains Whiplash. (When an enemy model misses a model with Whiplash with a magic attack, the attacking model becomes the target and is automatically hit by the attack. AOE magic attacks that miss are centered on the attacking model. The model with Whiplash is the point of origin for all these attacks.)						
BACKLASH	3	8	–	–	YES	YES
When target enemy warjack that is part of a battlegroup is damaged, its controller suffers 1 damage point.						
BANISHING WARD	2	6	–	–	YES	NO
Enemy upkeep spells on target friendly model/unit expire. Affected models cannot be targeted by enemy spells or animi.						
PHANTOM HUNTER	2	6	–	–	YES	NO
Target model in this model's battlegroup ignores LOS when making charges, slams, and attacks. That model ignores concealment and cover when resolving attacks.						
RIFT	3	8	4	13	NO	YES
The AOE is rough terrain and remains in play for one round.						

TACTICAL TIPS

The Vanishing – Models that cannot be charged cannot be slammed.

Phantom Hunter – Keep in mind that Phantom Seeker does not ignore Stealth.

Kaelyssa is the foremost strike force commander of the Retribution's mage hunters. She has a casual style of leadership that fosters genuine bonds with her subordinates balanced by an efficient professionalism, a razor-sharp mind, and a biting wit. In battle her hunters see a different side of her; she becomes a stalking predator with reflexes and situational awareness bordering on the preternatural. Her sergeants claim she can hear the heartbeats of the enemy and taste their movements on the wind. Under cover of darkness Kaelyssa hits the enemy hard, firing runebolts straight through solid walls to kill her prey before vanishing without a trace.

Outside of battle, to those who do not know her Kaelyssa's personality seems oddly informal and relaxed among so many hardened fanatics. What may be mistaken for impiety is actually a result of complete immersion in the cause. Her parents were sworn to the Retribution, and she was raised traveling among hidden cells. She regularly saw everyone around her put themselves in danger for their convictions and expects no less of herself. Kaelyssa's belief in Scyrah and the mage hunter way of life are as much a part of her as the marrow in her bones.

It was early in her mage hunter training that Kaelyssa manifested surprisingly powerful sorcerous abilities. This drew the attention of Shyeel arcanists aiding the Retribution. In fostering her ability they realized she had a particular knack for unraveling and deflecting flows of magic. Kaelyssa has smoothly integrated these powers into her strike style to become a truly formidable hunter. Those wizards caught in her sights are left defenseless as their own magic can be negated or turned against them.

The Retribution's regard for ability over seniority has allowed this child of the cause to rise rapidly in the ranks. She has had considerable success leading more than a dozen carefully orchestrated assaults abroad and eagerly anticipates the more ambitious operations planned for the future. She was recently entrusted to oversee the operational side of the Unseen Spear, home to the bulk of the sect's independent mage hunter strike teams. She refuses to accept even the possibility of failure.

To Kaelyssa her calling is a dangerous but thrilling endeavor, and with every mission she extends the depths of her talents. No one doubts her potential; it only remains to be seen how she will handle greater responsibilities and whether she can guide the Unseen Spear to leave a lasting legacy.

ADEPTIS RAHN
RETRIBUTION WARCASTER

Ambition. Power. Determination. The traits that define a strong ally also make for a formidable enemy. —Dawnlord Vyros

ADEPTIS RAHN						
SPD	STR	MAT	RAT	DEF	ARM	CMD
5	6	6	4	14	16	9

BALANCE	
POW	P+S
6	12

FOCUS	8
DAMAGE	16
FIELD ALLOWANCE	C
WARJACK POINTS	+6
SMALL BASE	

FEAT: ARCANE ALIGNMENT

Adeptis Rahn of House Shyeel is an expert controller of arcane force able to perceive energy as visible currents. In an ultimate demonstration of his supreme will, he seizes hold of these flows and aligns their energies to deliver an earth-sundering torrent of raw arcane power.

While in Rahn's control area, friendly Faction models gain +2 RNG to their non-channeled spells, and their magic attack rolls and magic attack damage rolls are boosted. Arcane Alignment lasts for one turn.

ADEPTIS RAHN

Force Barrier – This model gains +2 DEF against ranged attack rolls and does not suffer blast damage.

BALANCE

⊘ **Magical Weapon**

⊘ **Reach**

Beat Back – Immediately after a normal attack with this weapon is resolved during this model's combat action, the enemy model hit can be pushed 1″ directly away from the attacking model. After the enemy model is pushed, the attacking model can advance up to 1″.

Critical Smite – On a critical hit, this model can slam the model hit instead of rolling damage normally. The model hit is slammed d6″ directly away from this model and suffers a damage roll with POW equal to this model's STR plus the POW of this weapon. The POW of collateral damage is equal to this model's STR.

SPELLS	COST	RNG	AOE	POW	UP	OFF
CHAIN BLAST	3	10	3	12	NO	YES

After determining the point of impact for this attack, roll deviation for an additional 3″ AOE from that point. Models in that AOE are hit and suffer a POW 6 blast damage roll.

FORCE BLAST	3	CTRL	*	–	NO	NO

Target a model in this model's battlegroup in its control area. Enemy models within 2″ of the target model are pushed 4″ directly away from it in the order you choose.

FORCE FIELD	3	SELF	CTRL	–	YES	NO

This model does not suffer blast or collateral damage and cannot be knocked down. When an enemy AOE ranged attack deviates from a point in this model's control area, after the deviation distance is rolled you choose the deviation direction.

FORCE HAMMER	4	10	–	12	NO	YES

Instead of suffering a normal damage roll, a non-incorporeal model Force Hammer hits is slammed d6″ directly away from the spell's point of origin regardless of its base size and suffers a POW 12 damage roll. Collateral damage from this slam is POW 12.

POLARITY SHIELD	2	6	–	–	YES	NO

Target friendly model/unit cannot be targeted by a charge made by a model in its front arc.

TELEKINESIS	2	8	–	–	NO	*

Place target model completely within 2″ of its current location. When Telekinesis targets an enemy model, it is an offensive spell and requires a magic attack roll. A model can be affected by Telekinesis only once per turn.

TACTICAL TIPS

Beat Back – The attacking model can advance even if the enemy model is destroyed by the attack.

Critical Smite – Remember, the slammed model is moved only half the distance rolled if it has a larger base than the slamming model.

Force Hammer – Incorporeal models are not slammed. They just suffer a damage roll.

Polarity Shield – Remember, if a model cannot charge a target, it also cannot slam the target.

Among the most powerful arcanists born in a generation, Adeptis Rahn Shyeel is a master of force manipulation and arcane science. His movements send ripples through the air, and with but a thought he can generate storms of kinetic power capable of rending metal and bursting flesh. With a wave of his hand men and machines alike are swatted aside as easily as gnats, and it is just as effortlessly that he brushes away entire volleys of incoming fire. When he speaks, his words carry the palpable threat of his crushing will. He backs down to no one, no matter their rank, when it comes to matters he sees as his dominion.

Adeptis Rahn is a living embodiment of the battle mage discipline. With the control of raw force as his sphere of specialty, he has risen to a position of undisputed leadership. Some would say the field has left its imprint on his personality as well: Rahn Shyeel has an imperious demeanor and an unflinching temperament. He enters any

discussion as if it were a fight, choosing his words and ideas like weapons.

Rahn is arguably an even more influential representative of his house than Consul Hyselle, to whom he answers. The consul may stand among the Nine Voices, but it is the adeptis who directly commands the house's battle mages. It falls to him to demonstrate House Shyeel is an equal partner in the Retribution, sharing its risks and glories and not simply serving as a production source for myrmidons.

Although not an artificer, the adeptis nonetheless has great sway over the design and final shape of his house's myrmidons. Before openly joining the Retribution, Rahn frequently toured Ios' fortresses to test the effectiveness of myrmidon chassis for their intended roles. He established close ties to House Nyarr in listening to the needs of its officers and conveying them to the Shyeel ruling nobles.

Rahn is at heart a pragmatist. While he acknowledges Scyrah's condition and the peril represented by her eventual loss, he is not a true believer in the Retribution's cause. To him the organization is a convenient tool, a mechanism for societal change, and a lever to raise himself and his house to greater heights. This may seem selfish, but the sheer will and absolute self-confidence required to command the powers Rahn wields allows for nothing else. His philosophy is to control absolutely what is within his reach and ignore what is not. Scyrah will not die in the scope of his remaining years, so why trouble himself about her? Others are occupied with that task.

Adeptis Rahn's arcane expertise goes hand in hand with his ruthlessness. While some of his peers view combat as an unpleasant but unavoidable reality, Rahn is ever eager to march to war. The chaotic fluxes of violent energies and impulses that overtake the field have, to his eyes, an undeniable beauty. He relishes every moment he can spend in the maelstrom of battle.

RAVYN, ETERNAL LIGHT
RETRIBUTION WARCASTER

She is the very heart and soul of our struggle. —Orator Lysenne Bylvesh, Retribution priestess

RAVYN						
SPD	STR	MAT	RAT	DEF	ARM	CMD
6	6	7	7	15	16	9

HELLEBORE			
RNG	ROF	AOE	POW
12	1	—	12

BLADE	
POW	P+S
7	13

FOCUS	6
DAMAGE	16
FIELD ALLOWANCE	C
WARJACK POINTS	+6
SMALL BASE	

FEAT: FIRE STORM

Ravyn the Eternal Light can call on the blessings of Scyrah to instill her allies with singular devotion. Putting aside all distractions to annihilate the enemy, her forces advance forward as a storm of vengeance that will not be denied.

While in Ravyn's control area this turn, friendly Faction models gain boosted ranged attack rolls and Swift Hunter.

RAVYN

⟳ **Gunfighter**

Quick Work – When this model destroys one or more enemy models with a melee attack during its combat action, immediately after that attack is resolved this model can make one normal ranged attack. Attacks gained from Quick Work do not count against a weapon's ROF.

Swift Hunter – When this model destroys an enemy model with a normal ranged attack, immediately after the attack is resolved it can advance up to 2″.

Virtuoso – This model can make melee and ranged attacks during the same combat action. When this model makes its initial attacks, it can make both its initial ranged and melee attacks.

HELLEBORE

⊘ **Magical Weapon**

Blaster – When this model makes an attack with this weapon, before the attack roll it can spend 1 focus point to give the attack a 3″ AOE.

BLADE

⊘ **Magical Weapon**

⊘ **Reach**

Thresher (★Attack) – This model makes one melee attack with this weapon against each model in its LOS and this weapon's melee range.

Ravyn stands as a beacon of hope within a sect consumed by an apocalyptic vision of the future. She is widely admired both for her dedication to the goddess and for her unquestionable skill as a warrior and leader. Off the field she possesses a calm and pious wisdom. In battle some believe her to be invincible.

When this seasoned soldier enters the fray she holds back nothing. She enters a state of perfect detachment as she accepts the approach of death. Her weapon, Hellebore, becomes an extension of her will as she fires, strikes, and

SPELLS	COST	RNG	AOE	POW	UP	OFF
ELIMINATOR	3	8	3	13	NO	YES

Immediately after this attack is resolved, this model can advance up to 2″ for each enemy model destroyed by the attack.

LOCOMOTION	*	6	—	—	NO	NO

This model spends up to 3 focus points to cast Locomotion. Target warjack in this model's battlegroup immediately advances up to 1″ for each focus point spent. A warjack can be targeted by Locomotion only once per turn.

SNIPE	2	6	—	—	YES	NO

Target friendly model's/unit's ranged weapons gain +4 RNG.

VEIL OF MISTS	3	CTRL	4	—	YES	NO

Place a 4″ AOE cloud effect anywhere completely in this model's control area. This AOE does not block friendly Faction models' LOS. While in the AOE, friendly Faction models gain Pathfinder and can move through obstructions and other models if they have enough movement to move completely past them.

VORTEX OF DESTRUCTION	2	SELF	—	—	YES	NO

Damage rolls against enemy models in this model's melee range are automatically boosted.

TACTICAL TIPS

Thresher – The melee attacks are all simultaneous.

fires again. She sweeps through enemies in a whirling sequence of slashes and thrusts, each maneuver striking a mortal blow or leaving a maiming injury. She takes no joy in killing, but neither does she shrink from it. When Scyrah is restored, she plans to embrace peace as readily as she now welcomes war.

Ravyn spent most of her adult years in service to the Fane Knights and was one of few among them who fought to end the atrocities of House Vyre. Her small band took the forefront in a string of major battles and is credited with turning the tide in the north. With only ten knights, Ravyn defeated an army five hundred strong blockading the road between Lynshynal and Shyrr. She crashed her myrmidons through the barricade and carved her way through a sea of warriors to slay the blockade leaders. She personally ended the lives of dozens of high-ranking nobles and officers. The surviving army surrendered, and in the following weeks several enemy groups laid down their arms without a fight when Ravyn confronted them. She was heralded as a hero throughout Ios.

Five years ago Ravyn shocked her peers by leaving the Fane Knights to join the Retribution of Scyrah. Given her record of service, this decision was a serious blow to the fane. What outsiders did not realize was that this decision was not made hastily but came only after long deliberation prompted by several secret meetings between Ravyn and Orator Lysenne Bylvesh, second in command among the Retribution's clergy and one of the

Nine Voices. This former fane priestess persuaded Ravyn that the Retribution had ample evidence their war against humanity could restore Scyrah and that her energies were being squandered in the fane.

The Nine Voices bestowed on Ravyn the title of Eternal Light to represent the hope she embodies. She has been appointed their primary battlefield liaison and sent to lead the fight abroad. Despite her short history with the Retribution, her name is synonymous with service to Scyrah and Ios, thus this standing has been rapidly embraced. To many in the organization, Ravyn is seen as a fighting embodiment of the righteousness of their holy cause.

DAWNLORD VYROS
RETRIBUTION WARCASTER

In his eyes I see the glory of our house reborn. He will carve a path by blade's edge to our proper destiny. —Consul Caelcyr Nyarr

DAWNLORD VYROS

SPD	STR	MAT	RAT	DEF	ARM	CMD
5	7	8	4	15	17	10

JUSTICAR
POW	P+S
7	14

FOCUS	6
DAMAGE	18
FIELD ALLOWANCE	C
WARJACK POINTS	+6
SMALL BASE	

FEAT: PERFECT EXECUTION

To Dawnlord Vyros there is nothing more joyous than a precisely executed plan. With each enemy his forces destroy, Vyros imbues his myrmidons with escalating power until he sends them as a wall of metal to shatter the enemy's final resolve.

While in Vyros' control area this turn, when a friendly Faction model destroys an enemy model with an attack, allocate 1 focus point to a warjack in Vyros' battlegroup in his control area.

DAWNLORD VYROS

Bird's Eye – While in this model's control area, models in its battlegroup extend their front arcs 360° and when determining LOS ignore cloud effects, forest terrain, and intervening models.

Flank [Faction Warjack] – When this model makes a melee attack against an enemy model within the melee range of a friendly model of the listed type, this model gains +2 to attack rolls and gains an additional damage die.

JUSTICAR
- ⊘ Magical Weapon
- ⊘ Reach

SPELLS	COST	RNG	AOE	POW	UP	OFF
ELIMINATOR	3	8	3	13	NO	YES

Immediately after this attack is resolved, this model can advance up to 2˝ for each enemy model destroyed by the attack.

HALLOWED AVENGER	2	6	–	–	YES	NO

When an enemy attack destroys or removes from play one or more friendly Faction models within 5˝ of target warjack in this model's battlegroup, after the attack is resolved the affected warjack can charge an enemy model, then Hallowed Avenger expires.

INVIOLABLE RESOLVE	2	6	–	–	YES	NO

Target friendly Faction model/unit gains +2 ARM and Fearless.

MOBILITY	2	SELF	CTRL	–	NO	NO

Models in this model's battlegroup currently in its control area gain +2 SPD and Pathfinder for one turn.

STRANGLEHOLD	2	10	–	11	NO	YES

A model damaged by Stranglehold forfeits either its movement or its action during its next activation, as its controller chooses.

TACTICAL TIPS

Perfect Execution – A warjack cannot exceed normal focus allocation limits as a result of Perfect Execution.

Inviolable Resolve – Fleeing models immediately rally when affected by Inviolable Resolve.

Dawnlord Vyros is the heir presumptive of House Nyarr and thereby one of the most formidable individuals in Ios. That he is also a warcaster backed by the entire Dawnguard gives him military strength equal to his political clout. Few know the full extent of his ambitions, but his current actions are only the start of larger, more intricate machinations. Powerful allies stand ready to support him, including Adeptis Rahn Shyeel and his own uncle and house leader, Consul Caelcyr Nyarr. Vyros views the military might of the new Retribution as a sword in his hands, one sufficient to sunder any obstacle.

Vyros is the son of the Consul Caeclyr's younger brother Hylos, who died of a wasting disease long ago. While the aging consul has never explicitly addressed his succession, his nephew Vyros is the clear choice for heir. He has publicly expressed disinterest in the seat, but those who know him best realize there is no limit to his political ambitions and ruling his house is key to his future plans.

The dawnlord came to widespread attention for his pivotal role at the end of the War of the Houses, when he faced Ghyrrshyld in battle. It was during this clash that Vyros lost his eye, but even that grievous injury could not stop him from delivering what should have been a deathstroke. The mortally wounded Ghyrrshyld fled and somehow managed to delay his end long enough to transform into an eldritch. Over the years Vyros has sometimes brooded on seeking the opportunity to put a final end to this loathsome creature, a hope rekindled by recent events.

For now Vyros directs his energy toward consolidating his hold on the Retribution. He has the absolute loyalty of the Dawnguard, and his authority extends to the volunteered assets of dozens of other houses. Together with Adeptis Rahn Shyeel he also has influence over the disposition of myrmidons and battle mages.

The dawnlord has a reputation as a bold and forthright general who leads by example on and off the field. His men are proud to serve under his charge, as he embodies the principles he expects the Dawnguard to uphold, never wavering in his focus and dedication. Even seemingly trivial pursuits such as the noble sport of falconry Vyros extends to applications in war. Vyros has learned to link his mind to his hawk Jyren's, giving him the tactical advantage of looking down through her eyes to survey the battlefield.

To outside appearances Vyros is a selfless and heroic military commander, and he has worked to keep his larger ambitions private. He has endorsed the Retribution because he firmly believes Ios requires new leadership. Recovering Nyssor and restoring Scyrah may be the goals of the Retribution, but for him these are only the opening acts in a larger drama he hopes will result in the founding of a new and stronger elven empire—with Narcissar Vyros as its supreme ruler.

CHIMERA
RETRIBUTION LIGHT MYRMIDON

If the essence of the initiative is unpredictability and surprise, then the Chimera is a most perfect weapon of war.
—Adeptis Rahn Shyeel

CHIMERA						
SPD	STR	MAT	RAT	DEF	ARM	CMD
6	8	6	5	12	16	—

GLAIVE		
L	POW	P+S
	4	12

GLAIVE		
R	POW	P+S
	4	12

DAMAGE

1	2	3	4	5	6
		G	G		
	L	A	A	R	
L	L	M	C	R	R
	M	M	C	C	

FIELD DAMAGE	6
FIELD ALLOWANCE	U
POINT COST	6
MEDIUM BASE	

HEIGHT/WEIGHT: 9´1˝/2.4 TONS

ARMAMENT: GLAIVES (BOTH), PHANTASMAL FIELD (FIELD), APPARITION PROJECTOR GENERATOR (FIELD), ARC NODE

PEAK OPERATIONAL DURATION: 2 HRS COMBAT

ARTIFICER: HOUSE SHYEEL

CHIMERA

⊕ Arc Node

Apparition – During your Control Phase, place this model anywhere completely within 2˝ of its current location.

Field Dependent – While its Field Generator system is crippled, this model loses the Apparition and Phantasmal Field abilities.

Phantasmal Field – This model gains +1 DEF against ranged and magic attack rolls for each focus point on it.

GLAIVE

✊ Open Fist

Combo Strike (★Attack) – Make a melee attack. Instead of making a normal damage roll, the POW of the damage roll is equal to this model's STR plus twice the POW of this weapon.

The intricate components of the Chimera keep it in relatively limited production although the chassis is in high demand among the Retribution's few warcasters due to its arc node. Most Retribution warcasters prefer to enter battle backed by at least a pair of Chimeras and take more if available. Arc node technology represents a combat doctrine long ingrained in Iosan arcanists whereby extending a mage's power has been key to success in war. It was only natural that myrmidons would be put to such use, and the Chimera is the latest in a long line of machines refined toward that end.

TACTICAL TIPS

Combo Strike – Remember, this model cannot make a Combo Strike while either of its arm systems is locked or disabled.

The appearance of the Chimera has an unsettling impact on the enemies of the Retribution, for its active power field makes its form blur and fade, sometimes appearing to be several feet from where it actually stands. Even at rest these generators give the myrmidon an impression of shifting movement, and it can be difficult to pin down. Once it nears the enemy, a Chimera becomes a delivery device for its warcaster's most powerful arcane powers channeled across its arc node. The Chimera will strike and kill with its scything arm-mounted glaives then vanish as nearby soldiers turn desperately to engage it. With a flicker of blended light it appears behind them to deliver arcane death.

GORGON
RETRIBUTION LIGHT MYRMIDON

The Gorgon works on the principle that nothing is so disheartening to an enemy leader as being deprived of the ability to engage on his terms. —Battle Mage Magister Jysorven of House Shyeel

The Gorgon exists to dictate the flow of battle by depriving the enemy of mobility. Its core technologies involve manipulating and generating powerful kinetic fields. Its integral force cannon unleashes blasts of raw energy capable of forestalling an enemy's forward momentum, offering a substantial ranged threat that also serves to throw an enemy off its stride. Its more powerful fields require close proximity, and the Gorgon will rush forward to seize hold of even larger and more powerful 'jacks or myrmidons to pin them in place as its energy field sparks and thrums with raw power. While its force-locked prey struggles to extract itself, the Gorgon deals punishing blows with its arm-mounted glaives, capable of tearing apart even the strongest steel.

GORGON

Field Dependent – While its Field Generator system is crippled, this model loses the Force Lock ability and cannot make Polarity Cannon attacks.

Force Lock – Enemy models in this model's melee range cannot advance except to change facing.

POLARITY CANNON

⚙ **Magical Weapon**

Kinetic Grip – When a model is hit by this attack, it cannot charge this model for one round.

GLAIVE

✊ **Open Fist**

Combo Strike (★Attack) – Make a melee attack. Instead of making a normal damage roll, the POW of the damage roll is equal to this model's STR plus twice the POW of this weapon.

GORGON

SPD	STR	MAT	RAT	DEF	ARM	CMD
6	8	6	5	12	16	—

POLARITY CANNON

RNG	ROF	AOE	POW
10	1	—	10

GLAIVE (L)

POW	P+S
4	12

GLAIVE (R)

POW	P+S
4	12

DAMAGE

1	2	3	4	5	6
	L	G	G	R	
L	L	M	C	R	R
M	M	C	C		

FIELD DAMAGE	6
FIELD ALLOWANCE	U
POINT COST	5

MEDIUM BASE

HEIGHT/WEIGHT: 9´/2.25 TONS

ARMAMENT: GLAIVES (BOTH), POLARITY CANNON (FIELD), FORCE LOCK GENERATOR (FIELD)

PEAK OPERATIONAL DURATION: 2.25 HRS COMBAT

ARTIFICER: HOUSE SHYEEL

Perfecting these force manipulation technologies required several decades of refinement by House Shyeel artificers. This required certain sophisticated power field manipulations to create the equivalent of a kinetic anchor, a field that could seize nearby matter and keep it locked in place. The Gorgon's success required a particularly high-yield energy generator for such a small chassis. Certain power innovations made during the development of the Gorgon would later be applied to other chassis, greatly increasing power efficiency of all Shyeel myrmidons.

TACTICAL TIPS

Kinetic Grip – Remember that if a model cannot charge, it also cannot slam.

Combo Strike – Remember, this model cannot make a Combo Strike while either of its arm systems is locked or disabled.

GRIFFON
RETRIBUTION LIGHT MYRMIDON

As unencumbered as the wind, the Griffon moves freely to strike at the time and place of our choosing. —Invictor Captain Chysor

GRIFFON						
SPD	STR	MAT	RAT	DEF	ARM	CMD
6	8	6	5	12	16	—

SHIELD	
POW	P+S
1	9

L

HALBERD	
POW	P+S
5	13

R

DAMAGE

1	2	3	4	5	6

L	G	G	R
L	L	M	C	R	R
M	M	C	C

FIELD DAMAGE	6
FIELD ALLOWANCE	U
POINT COST	4
MEDIUM BASE	

HEIGHT/WEIGHT: 9´/2.6 TONS

ARMAMENT: HALBERD (RIGHT), SHIELD (LEFT), KINETIC CONVERSION DRIVE (FIELD)

PEAK OPERATIONAL DURATION: 3 HRS COMBAT

ARTIFICER: HOUSE SHYEEL

GRIFFON
🜂 Pathfinder

Field Dependent – While its Field Generator system is crippled, this model loses the Pathfinder and Fleet abilities.

Fleet – At the start of this model's activation, it can spend 1 focus point once to gain +2˝ movement for one turn.

SHIELD
+2 Shield

HALBERD
⟳ Reach

Powerful Charge – This model gains +2 to charge attack rolls with this weapon.

The Griffon's great durability and long peak operational time make it a desirable asset, and its relatively simple component parts make it easy and inexpensive to produce. It represents a small enough resource investment that it is liberally allocated to officers trained to control it. House Shyeel produces them in great numbers to supply this wide use; it has, in fact, constructed almost twice as many Griffons as any other myrmidon. With a proven effectiveness as part of both Dawnguard and mage hunter armies, the Griffon provides invaluable support and striking power to the infantry it fights alongside, whatever force it joins.

The Griffon is a sleek and fast myrmidon designed for rapid battlefield deployment and swift flanking maneuvers. Its power field enables the Griffon to become near-weightless for short intervals, allowinging for long, loping strides with impossibly long pauses at the apex of each leap. Through judicious use of this field the Griffon can negotiate marshy terrain, dense undergrowth, or other obstacles that would mire machines of similar weight. It is used to sweep around enemy entrenchments to assault them from the rear or to hit perceived weak points in the enemy line. It is often sent rushing ahead of the main line to intercept an enemy in advance of the main Iosan battle force.

HYDRA
RETRIBUTION HEAVY MYRMIDON

That which does not cut us down fuels our resolve. —Adeptis Jyre Srensyr

The Hydra is singularly self reliant in the field, for it can convert raw kinetic energy from the force of incoming attacks into a firestorm of retributive destruction. Enhanced with force generators integrated into its mighty fists, the Hydra can unleash a torrent of crushing blows before tossing aside even the most massive of adversaries. Excess energy is stored in a series of arcane batteries that greatly enhance the power of the myrmidon's attacks.

Once it is powered, the Hydra's great reserves of energy last until expended, making it a favorite myrmidon in the Retribution's wars abroad. Experienced commanders fortunate enough to control Hydras in battle make it a top priority to ensure the machines are fully powered at the onset of hostilities. Once joined in battle, the myrmidon often needs little more than mental guidance from its controlling warcaster, for its vitality is continually restored by oncoming attacks.

HYDRA

Field Dependent – While its Field Generator system is crippled, this model loses the Kinetic Capacitor ability and cannot attack with the Force Cannon.

Focus Battery – During the Maintenance Phase, do not remove unspent focus points from this model. Focus points remaining on this model at the start of your Control Phase count toward its focus allocation limit.

Kinetic Capacitor – When this model is hit by an enemy melee or ranged attack, after the attack is resolved this model gains 1 focus point.

FORCE CANNON

⊘ **Magical Weapon**

Focus Powered – For each focus point on this model when it declares an attack with this weapon, the weapon gains +1 RNG and +1 POW for the rest of the attack.

FORCE FIST

✊ **Open Fist**

Chain Attack: Grab & Smash – If this model hits the same model with both its initial attacks with this weapon, after resolving the attacks it can immediately make a double-hand throw, head-butt, head/weapon/arm lock, push, or throw power attack against that target.

HYDRA						
SPD	STR	MAT	RAT	DEF	ARM	CMD
6	10	6	5	12	18	—

FORCE CANNON			
RNG	ROF	AOE	POW
12	1	—	12

FORCE FIST	
POW	P+S
4	14

FORCE FIST	
POW	P+S
4	14

DAMAGE

1	2	3	4	5	6
		□	□		
	□	□	□	□	
	L	G	G	R	
L	L	M	C	R	R
M	M	C	C		

FIELD DAMAGE	10
FIELD ALLOWANCE	U
POINT COST	9
LARGE BASE	

HEIGHT/WEIGHT: 12´2˝/5.25 TONS

ARMAMENT: FORCE FISTS (BOTH), FORCE CANNON (FIELD), KINETIC CAPACITOR (FIELD), FOCUS BATTERY

PEAK OPERATIONAL DURATION: 2.5 HRS COMBAT

ARTIFICER: HOUSE SHYEEL

TACTICAL TIPS

Focus Powered – The bonus to RNG and POW is applied when an attack is declared with this weapon, before attack or damage rolls. This means that if this model spends focus to boost its attack or damage roll, the bonuses still apply.

MANTICORE
RETRIBUTION HEAVY MYRMIDON

In battle, there are not more than two methods of attack—the direct and the indirect—yet these two in combination give rise to an endless series of maneuvers. —Ossyris, the Sovereign of Conflict

MANTICORE						
SPD	STR	MAT	RAT	DEF	ARM	CMD
6	10	6	5	12	18	—

CYCLONE CANNON			
RNG	ROF	AOE	POW
12	3	—	12

SABER FIST	
POW	P+S
L	
5	15

SABER FIST	
POW	P+S
R	
5	15

DAMAGE

1	2	3	4	5	6

	L	G	G	R	
L	L	M	C	R	R
	M	M	C	C	

FIELD DAMAGE	10
FIELD ALLOWANCE	U
POINT COST	8
LARGE BASE	

MANTICORE

Field Dependent – While its Field Generator system is crippled, this model loses the Force Generator ability, cannot attack with the Cyclone Cannon, and cannot make Covering Fire special actions.

Force Generator – At the start of this model's activation, it can spend 1 focus point once to gain +3 STR for one turn.

CYCLONE CANNON

Ⓜ **Magical Weapon**

Covering Fire (★Action) – Place a 3″ AOE anywhere completely within this weapon's RNG. The center point of the AOE must be in this model's LOS, ignoring intervening models. A model entering or ending its activation in the AOE suffers a damage roll with POW equal to the POW of this weapon. The AOE remains in play for one round or until this model is destroyed or removed from play.

SABER FIST

✊ **Open Fist**

Combo Strike (★Attack) – Make a melee attack. Instead of making a normal damage roll, the POW of the damage roll is equal to this model's STR plus twice the POW of this weapon.

HEIGHT/WEIGHT: 12′2″/5.3 TONS

ARMAMENT: SABER FISTS (BOTH), CYCLONE CANNON (FIELD), FORCE GENERATOR (FIELD)

PEAK OPERATIONAL DURATION: 3 HRS COMBAT

ARTIFICER: HOUSE SHYEEL

cannon, a force weapon fueled by the same generator that powers its kinetic field. This dual capacity gives the Manticore tremendous versatility in tactics, and it has proven its worth in a wide variety of battlefield situations.

The rapid-fire cannon is a true terror to the enemies of the Retribution. The weapon can lay down suppressive fire to support advances or be concentrated into volleys to tear apart several targets at range. The combination of the Manticore's brutal power and its flexible ranged support make it a mainstay in the Retribution's arsenal. This go-to myrmidon is expected to be produced and fielded in quantity.

TACTICAL TIPS

Combo Strike – Remember, this model cannot make a Combo Strike while either of its arm systems is locked or disabled.

Driven by the kinetic force of its field generator, the Manticore is among the most physically powerful of all Iosan myrmidons. In combat it stalks the battlefield like a force of nature, savage and unforgiving in its ferocity. Its every thunderous blow is transformed into an explosion of earth-shaking power. Bolstering its formidable physical strength is the myrmidon's cyclone

PHOENIX
RETRIBUTION HEAVY MYRMIDON

In our darkest hour we will ignite such a fire that the whole world will be purified in its radiance. —Oracle Relvinor Luynmyr

In battle the Phoenix becomes a blazing embodiment of Iosan power. Its blinding power field pours blue-white heat into its surroundings as liquid fire ignites along its massive thermal blade. It is a myrmidon designed to be a supreme weapon of war, in particular one that would be worthy of the Dawnguard and stand as a clearly visible embodiment of their order. It has been quickly accepted within the larger Retribution military and has earned a reputation as a premier myrmidon well worth its cost to produce.

The Phoenix was designed to deliver its arc node directly to the heart of the enemy. It extends a warcaster's reach and therefore his power on the battlefield, yet it does so in a distinctly different fashion than the elusive Chimera. The Phoenix has the durability and power to advance at the vanguard of an attacking force, ready to deliver fiery retaliation on any enemy foolish enough to try to intercept it. Its blazing power field regenerates itself in the course of combat and can send a surge of energy to ignite the surrounding air and burn its enemies to ash. In the Phoenix, House Shyeel has created a formidable and elegantly designed masterpiece of warfare. To its enemies the Phoenix represents something else: a terrifying apparition of fiery steel embodying the rage of the Retribution of Scyrah.

PHOENIX
- **⊕ Arc Node**

Combustion (★Attack) – Models within 2″ of this model suffer a POW 12 fire damage roll and the Fire continuous effect. This model can make additional melee attacks after making this special attack.

Field Dependent – While its Field Generator system is crippled, this model loses the Phoenix Field ability and cannot attack with the Halo Cannon.

Phoenix Field – Remove d6 damage points from this model's force field after resolving continuous effects during your Maintenance Phase.

HALO CANNON
- **⊛ Critical Fire**
- **🔥 Damage Type: Fire**
- **⊘ Magical Weapon**

OPEN FIST
- **✊ Open Fist**

THERMAL BLADE
- **⊘ Magical Weapon**
- **⊛ Continuous Effect: Fire**
- **↻ Reach**

PHOENIX						
SPD	STR	MAT	RAT	DEF	ARM	CMD
6	10	6	5	12	18	—

HALO CANNON			
RNG	ROF	AOE	POW
10	1	3	14

OPEN FIST	
POW	P+S
3	13

THERMAL BLADE	
POW	P+S
7	17

DAMAGE

1	2	3	4	5	6
		G	G		
	L	A	A	R	
L	L	M	C	R	R
	M	M	C	C	

FIELD DAMAGE	10
FIELD ALLOWANCE	**U**
POINT COST	**10**
LARGE BASE	

HEIGHT/WEIGHT: 13′4″/6.5 TONS

ARMAMENT: THERMAL BLADE (RIGHT ARM), HALO CANNON (FIELD), PHOENIX FIELD (FIELD), ARC NODE

PEAK OPERATIONAL DURATION: 2.25 HRS COMBAT

ARTIFICER: HOUSE SHYEEL

TACTICAL TIPS
Combustion – This model cannot use Combustion if it charges because Combustion is not a melee attack.

DAWNGUARD INVICTORS
RETRIBUTION UNIT

Those who would call themselves Dawnguard must excel in every facet of war. —Dawnlord Vyros Nyarr

LEADER & GRUNTS						
SPD	STR	MAT	RAT	DEF	ARM	CMD
5	6	7	7	12	15	9

SWORD CANNON			
RNG	ROF	AOE	POW
10	1	—	12

BLADE	
POW	P+S
4	10

FIELD ALLOWANCE	2
LEADER AND 5 GRUNTS	**6**
LEADER AND 9 GRUNTS	**10**
SMALL BASE	

LEADER & GRUNTS

⊘ **Combined Ranged Attack**

✪ **'Jack Marshal**

Defensive Line – While this model is B2B with one or more models in its unit, it gains +2 ARM.

Flank [Faction Warjack] – When this model makes a melee attack against an enemy model within the melee range of a friendly model of the listed type, this model gains +2 to attack rolls and gains an additional damage die.

of every major engagement where the Dawnguard are called to war, being the first to fire, the first to engage, and the first to endure the brunt of an enemy attack.

Over the last several centuries, myrmidons have become an increasingly vital aspect of House Nyarr's battle doctrine. Invictors drill endlessly alongside the myrmidons, mastering a vast number of tactics and support maneuvers. Invictor commanders are sometimes awarded their own myrmidons as a mark of distinction. Griffons are particularly well-regarded by invictors who serve with them in the field.

Invictors make up the bulk of House Nyarr's Dawnguard order. Prized for unrelenting versatility, the Invictors are a heavy infantry force unlike any other on the face of Caen. When supported by the formidable Iosan myrmidons, invictors are unsurpassed on the battlefield. Firing their weapons as they close, invictors are ever ready to charge into the ranks of the enemy and cut them down with the heavy blades set into their rifles.

Founded in the days of ancient Lyoss as an auxiliary for the Dawnguard Sentinels and Destors, the Invictors have slowly grown to become the mainstay of the Dawnguard. As weaponry and tactics evolved over the centuries, their role gradually expanded. Sentinels remain the premiere shock troopers of the Dawnguard, but because invictors are as deadly at range as they are in melee, they fulfill a broader number of roles. In fact most Dawnguard fortifications are garrisoned exclusively by Invictor forces. They now stand at the forefront

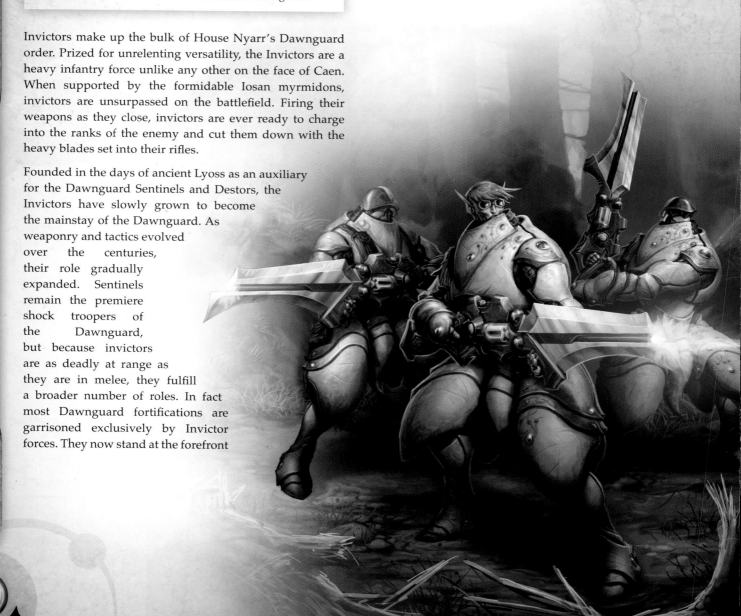

A soldier's purpose is to deliver death. It is a heavy responsibility. Honor your own life by honing your skill at war. Honor your people by choosing when to put that skill to use. —Ossyris, the Sovereign of Conflict

Peerless officers, invictor captains are seasoned veterans who have endured long years of service under equally merciless superiors. Each is responsible for the oversight of hundreds of subordinates. Their devotion to their order is as powerful and absolute as a priest's piety. Each captain has sworn to live and die with his weapon at the ready and has vowed that the successful completion of his orders will always be his first priority.

These leaders measure success by the performance of their companies as a whole and care less about individual heroics. Invictor captains therefore encourage camaraderie and cooperation over individual accomplishment. This applies both in success as well as failure, so the failures of one are also the failures of the company. Those who seek glory while endangering their peers are shamed in the same manner as those who fail to perform resolutely in battle. Though these officers are stern and unforgiving, they are also willing to fight tooth and nail to defend the veterans of their squads.

TACTICAL TIPS

Officer – Because this model is an Officer, it is the unit 'Jack Marshal while it is in play. When it is destroyed it does not replace a grunt in its unit. Instead the unit leader becomes the new unit commander and 'Jack Marshal.

Attachment [Dawnguard Invictors] – This attachment can be added to a unit of the type listed.

OFFICER

Ⓟ **Combined Ranged Attack**

Ⓢ **Officer**

Defensive Line – While this model is B2B with one or more models in its unit, it gains +2 ARM.

Extended Fire – Once per game while in formation, this model can use Extended Fire during its unit's activation. This activation, models in this unit gain +4 RNG to their ranged attacks.

Flank [Faction Warjack] – When this model makes a melee attack against an enemy model within the melee range of a friendly model of the listed type, this model gains +2 to attack rolls and gains an additional damage die.

Granted: Combined Arms – While this model is in play, models in its unit gain Combined Arms. (When a model with Combined Arms misses an attack roll for a combined ranged attack, it can reroll that attack roll. Each attack roll can be rerolled only once as a result of Combined Arms).

STANDARD BEARER

Ⓢ **Standard Bearer**

Defensive Line – While this model is B2B with one or more models in its unit, it gains +2 ARM.

OFFICER						
SPD	STR	MAT	RAT	DEF	ARM	CMD
5	6	8	7	12	15	10

SWORD CANNON			
RNG	ROF	AOE	POW
10	1	—	12

BLADE	
POW	P+S
4	10

STANDARD BEARER						
SPD	STR	MAT	RAT	DEF	ARM	CMD
5	6	7	6	12	15	9

OFFICER'S DAMAGE	5
FIELD ALLOWANCE	1
POINT COST	2
SMALL BASE	

All invictors are extensively drilled and trained to take part in complex coordinated actions, and this is particularly true of the veterans chosen to accompany each captain. Invictors move with frightening fluidity, instinctively following every order passed down to them by their captain. Relying on this discipline, invictor officers can deliver devastating concentrated fire at unprecedented range.

DAWNGUARD SENTINELS
RETRIBUTION UNIT

I pledge myself to eternal vigilance, swearing that the honor of our house shall live in the steel of my blade.
Let our watch stand unbroken. —Oath of the Dawnguard Sentinels

LEADER & GRUNTS						
SPD	STR	MAT	RAT	DEF	ARM	CMD
5	6	7	4	12	15	9

GREAT SWORD	
POW	P+S
6	12

FIELD ALLOWANCE	2
LEADER AND 5 GRUNTS	6
LEADER AND 9 GRUNTS	9
SMALL BASE	

LEADER & GRUNTS
⊛ 'Jack Marshal

Defensive Line – While this model is B2B with one or more models in its unit, it gains +2 ARM.

GREAT SWORD
⊘ Reach

ⓟ Weapon Master

Dawnguard Sentinels charge into the enemy as an overwhelming tide of cleaving blades. These heavily armored knights use their great swords expertly to carve through any adversary willing to stand against them. Sentinels are resolute even in the face of overwhelming casualties, willing to fight to the last to defend the pride of the Dawnguard. They embody sheer determination made tangible in flesh and steel.

Dawnguard Sentinels view themselves as the timeless essence of their order. They are inheritors and protectors of an ancient legacy dating back to their revered predecessors who died to save the Lyossan refugees during the desert crossing after the Cataclysm. There is undeniable prestige associated with these heavily armored infantry who are chosen from the strongest and most resolute of House Nyarr's noble youths. They are trained and disciplined for decades to serve in battle and stand ready to offer their lives for their kin. Sentinels have a keen sense of destiny and obligation to family and order, for they see the two as identical.

Eternal vigilance is their watchword. Sentinels consider themselves guardians of the ideals of the Dawnguard, and they strive to maintain doctrinal purity. Some might accuse the Sentinels of being obsessed with rituals and ceremony when compared with the Invictors, but they consider these symbolic gestures essential to their purpose. Their doctrine insists the safety of Ios requires readiness to march against any foe while fearing neither death nor destruction. Sentinels do not wait atop battlements for the enemy to approach; they rush forth to confront the foe directly.

DAWNGUARD SENTINEL OFFICER & STANDARD
RETRIBUTION UNIT ATTACHMENT

My soldiers are my blood. Every drop spilled shall be answered tenfold. —Oath of the Dawnguard Sentinel Officers

Sentinel captains are among the most disciplined and dedicated of the Dawnguard, and they will commit any action that will bring honor and glory to the order and thereby to House Nyarr. The Sentinel discipline is the one most often chosen by heirs of House Nyarr's bloodline, for it ensures that warriors of noble birth exemplify Dawnguard virtues.

Educated from an early age, noble youths are steeped in Dawnguard tradition. They begin training to wield the blade as soon as they are strong enough to lift it. Their lives become a constant repetition of practice, conditioning, drilling, study, and instruction in how to fulfill their obligations to the order and their house. These officers view soldiery as an essential way of life, and from birth they are prepared for leadership.

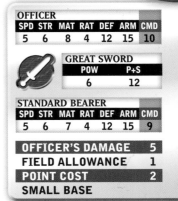

Attachment [Dawnguard Sentinels] – This attachment can be added to a unit of the type listed.

OFFICER

◎ Officer

Defensive Line – While this model is B2B with one or more models in its unit, it gains +2 ARM.

Drive: Pronto – This model can attempt to Drive each warjack under its control in its command range. To Drive a warjack, this model must make a command check at any time during its activation. If the check succeeds, the warjack immediately makes a full advance. If the check fails, the warjack does not benefit from 'Jack Marshal this turn.

Granted: Vengeance – While this model is in play, models in its unit gain Vengeance. (During your Maintenance Phase, if one or more models in a unit with Vengeance were destroyed or removed from play by enemy attacks during your opponent's last turn, each model in the unit can advance 3˝ and make one normal melee attack.)

STANDARD BEARER

🏳 Standard Bearer

Defensive Line – While this model is B2B with one or more models in its unit, it gains +2 ARM.

GREAT SWORD

⊘ Reach

🕃 Weapon Master

OFFICER						
SPD	STR	MAT	RAT	DEF	ARM	CMD
5	6	8	4	12	15	10

GREAT SWORD		
	POW	P+S
	6	12

STANDARD BEARER						
SPD	STR	MAT	RAT	DEF	ARM	CMD
5	6	7	4	12	15	9

OFFICER'S DAMAGE	5
FIELD ALLOWANCE	1
POINT COST	2
SMALL BASE	

TACTICAL TIPS

Officer –Because this model is an Officer, it is the unit 'Jack Marshal while it is in play. When it is destroyed it does not replace a grunt in its unit. Instead the unit leader becomes the new unit commander and 'Jack Marshal.

Unshakable loyalty and devotion to core Dawnguard principles define Sentinel officers. Banner bearers carry aloft in imperishable metal the oaths by which they live as a visible reminder to all their men of their purpose.

DAWNGUARD DESTORS
RETRIBUTION CAVALRY UNIT

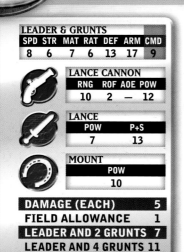

LEADER & GRUNTS						
SPD	STR	MAT	RAT	DEF	ARM	CMD
8	6	7	6	13	17	9

LANCE CANNON			
RNG	ROF	AOE	POW
10	2	—	12

LANCE	
POW	P+S
7	13

MOUNT
POW
10

DAMAGE (EACH)	5
FIELD ALLOWANCE	1
LEADER AND 2 GRUNTS	7
LEADER AND 4 GRUNTS	11
LARGE BASE	

LEADER & GRUNTS

Gunfighter

Dual Shot – When this model forfeits its movement to gain the aiming bonus it can also make one additional ranged attack this activation.

Unyielding – While engaging an enemy model, this model gains +2 ARM.

LANCE

Lance – This weapon can be used only to make charge attacks. When this model charges, this weapon gains reach until the charge is resolved.

TACTICAL TIPS

Gunfighter – Gunfighter does not enable models in this unit to make melee and ranged attack during the same activation.

Dual Shot – This is how the model gets to take the second shot allowed by the ROF 2 of its weapon.

Destors are the elite cavalry of the Dawnguard and now of the Retribution. They are used in support of massive infantry offensives to strike where the enemy line is weakest. Once they have penetrated the enemy line, the Destors wheel about and open fire with their lance cannons, an ingenious weapon created specifically for this branch of the order. The cannons allow the Destors to fire with surpassing accuracy even while at a full gallop across the battlefield. Destors stand ready to fell their enemies through deadly firepower or under their thunderous and crushing charge.

The Dawnguard is first and foremost known for its heavy infantry, and the Destors have always been far fewer in number than its knights on foot. They represent a respected if underrepresented branch of the order. Those drawn to this life embrace their standing and work tirelessly to prove their strengths on the battlefield. Firing accurately from horseback is extremely difficult and requires considerable practice even for those with talent. In testament to their abilities, Destors are sent to cripple and destroy hard targets among the enemy or to shatter crucial elements of the opposing line.

HOUSE SHYEEL BATTLE MAGES
RETRIBUTION UNIT

Force is not an abstract principle but a manifestation of our will. —Adeptis Rahn Shyeel

While battle mages may arise from other houses, only House Shyeel has made their exercise a military science. It has assembled numerous squads of arcanists trained to wield their powers as weapons. These mages have eschewed esoteric research into inconsequential magic theory in order to specialize in the application of raw evoked force. They are often as stern and direct as the magic they employ, and it has earned them an ominous reputation.

Battle mages practice a hybrid of the arcane and martial disciplines, and their training for physical combat refines their mental control over their powers. They have no fear of closing with the enemy, for they enter battle equipped with massive arcanika-charged gauntlets that lend supernatural

LEADER & GRUNTS

Force Barrier – This model gains +2 DEF against ranged attack rolls and does not suffer blast damage.

MAGIC ABILITY [6]

- **Force Bolt (★Attack)** – Force Bolt is a RNG 10, POW 10 magic attack. An enemy model hit by this attack may be pushed d3 inches directly toward or away from this model. On a critical hit, the enemy model is also knocked down after being pushed.

POWER GAUNTLETS

🔘 **Magical Weapon**

Beat Back – Immediately after a normal attack with this weapon is resolved during this model's combat action, the enemy model hit can be pushed 1˝ directly away from the attacking model. After the enemy model is pushed, the attacking model can advance up to 1˝.

LEADER & GRUNTS						
SPD	STR	MAT	RAT	DEF	ARM	CMD
6	7	6	4	13	12	9

POWER GAUNTLETS	
POW	P+S
4	11

FIELD ALLOWANCE	2
LEADER AND 5 GRUNTS	**5**
SMALL BASE	

strength to their strikes. Their arcane control over kinetic energies allows them to deflect incoming missile fire and emerge unscathed from the shrapnel of massive explosions.

House Shyeel has strategically deployed these mages throughout the armies of the Retribution to involve the house in all major operations. House leaders are not content to wait in Ios while sending myrmidons to support the Dawnguard. Battle mages represent Shyeel on the front lines where they earn their share of glory and preserve house interests. Some have suggested this is one step toward House Shyeel becoming a Great Military House. Thanks to the political opportunities opened by public support for the Retribution and the alliance with House Nyarr, these battle mages may succeed and usher in a new era of influence.

TACTICAL TIPS

Beat Back – The attacking model can advance even if the enemy model is destroyed by the attack.

HOUSEGUARD HALBERDIERS
RETRIBUTION UNIT

Others speak of sacrifice, yet it is our dead who will litter the field by nightfall and our banner that will stand atop the hill to shout defiance when our voices are silent. —House Syllrynal Halberdier Sergeant

LEADER & GRUNTS						
SPD	STR	MAT	RAT	DEF	ARM	CMD
6	5	6	4	13	14	8

HALBERD	
POW	P+S
5	10

FIELD ALLOWANCE	3
LEADER AND 5 GRUNTS	4
LEADER AND 9 GRUNTS	7
SMALL BASE	

LEADER & GRUNTS

⊘ **Combined Melee Attack**

Ranked Attacks – Friendly Faction models can ignore this model when determining LOS.

Shield Wall (Order) – For one round, each affected model gains a +4 ARM bonus while B2B with another affected model in its unit. This bonus does not apply to damage originating in the model's back arc. Models in this unit can begin the game affected by Shield Wall.

HALBERD

⊘ **Reach**

Brutal Charge – This model gains +2 to charge attack damage rolls with this weapon.

Set Defense – A model in this model's front arc suffers –2 on charge, slam power attack, and impact attack rolls against this model.

Houseguard forces have served in the defense of Ios since its foundation, and halberdiers in particular maintain an unbroken martial tradition predating Lyoss itself. Even in the hands of a fresh recruit, the halberd is a deadly weapon; the majority of the houseguard are career soldiers who have spent years at drill and formation. They know every cadence march and maneuver by heart. Disciplined ranks of halberdiers form a tide of rising and falling steel that can cut down masses of enemies with deliberate ease.

Because their numbers are drawn from disparate lesser Iosan households, there are noticeable variances in the uniforms and armor among the halberdiers, but their basic armament remains consistent and is based on ancient tradition. The manpower of the houseguard is what enables the Retribution to engage in battle against the armies of the human kingdoms. It is a grim fact of war that these companies, the army's lifeblood, will endure heavy losses in battles ahead. Halberdiers embrace this grim fact with pride as soldiers of the line.

HOUSEGUARD HALBERDIER OFFICER & STANDARD
RETRIBUTION UNIT ATTACHMENT

Remember the pride of your house, of your ancestors, as we fight against those who would annihilate our future. —Houseguard Arsyr Norcyl

Houseguard halberdiers are first and foremost professional soldiers practicing a long and honored tradition. The officers who lead these companies see themselves as consummate warriors and living examples for their subordinates. Most of these officers once served the Homeguard Coalition and drilled endlessly at both border and interior garrisons. They have replaced safe routine with the uncertainties of war and risking their lives on foreign soil. For these officers this is the chance to serve as they always intended, putting to practice skills and tactics otherwise unused. For many there is the incentive of playing a part in a cause they consider holy and necessary.

The companies brought into the Retribution military have joined for a variety of reasons, and this is reflected in their officers. Some serve from loyalty to house nobles who donated soldiers to the Retribution as a sign of solidarity. Others put aside former affiliations while caught up in the

TACTICAL TIPS

Officer – Remember this model can issue the Shield Wall order to its unit. Because this model is an Officer, when it is destroyed it does not replace a grunt in its unit. Instead the unit leader becomes the unit commander.

Attachment [Houseguard Halberdiers] – This attachment can be added to a unit of the type listed.

OFFICER

⊘ **Combined Melee Attack**

⊛ **Officer**

Granted: Reform – While this model is in play, after all models in its unit have completed their actions, each can advance up to 3˝.

Ranked Attacks – Friendly Faction models can ignore this model when determining LOS.

Team Effort – Once per game while in formation, this model can use this ability during its unit's activation. This activation, models in this unit gain +2 to attack and damage rolls when making a melee attack targeting an enemy model in melee range of another model in this unit.

STANDARD BEARER

⊘ **Standard Bearer**

HALBERD

⊘ **Reach**

Brutal Charge – This model gains +2 to charge attack damage rolls with this weapon.

Set Defense – A model in this model's front arc suffers –2 on charge, slam power attack, and impact attack rolls against this model.

OFFICER						
SPD	STR	MAT	RAT	DEF	ARM	CMD
6	5	7	4	13	14	9

HALBERD		
	POW	P+S
	5	10

STANDARD BEARER						
SPD	STR	MAT	RAT	DEF	ARM	CMD
6	5	6	4	13	14	8

OFFICER'S DAMAGE	5
FIELD ALLOWANCE	1
POINT COST	2
SMALL BASE	

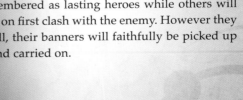

fervor spreading across Ios. While some companies remain tight-knit groups with close kinship ties, others comprise volunteers gathered across several houses and placed under a single strong and competent leader.

As officers inevitably fall in battle, chances will emerge for others to rise through the ranks to take their places. These officers must forge their men into disciplined groups acting as a single concerted body. In time some few will be remembered as lasting heroes while others will die on first clash with the enemy. However they fall, their banners will faithfully be picked up and carried on.

HOUSEGUARD RIFLEMEN
RETRIBUTION UNIT

Let our swordsmen and halberdiers be left idle and discontented as our foe drops, one after the next, dozens of yards short of their positions. —Rifleman Thane Tynsylas of House Nyvos

LEADER & GRUNTS						
SPD	STR	MAT	RAT	DEF	ARM	CMD
6	4	5	5	13	13	8

LONG RIFLE			
RNG	ROF	AOE	POW
14	1	—	10

SWORD	
POW	P+S
3	7

FIELD ALLOWANCE	3
LEADER AND 5 GRUNTS	5
LEADER AND 9 GRUNTS	8
SMALL BASE	

LEADER & GRUNTS

⊘ **Combined Ranged Attack**

Ranked Attacks – Friendly Faction models can ignore this model when determining LOS.

The collective defense of Ios has been a burden shouldered not solely by the Five Great Military Houses but by every citizen. The most vital element of this common defense was the large numbers of riflemen ready to fire on any approaching enemy from a great distance. Companies of these same riflemen have joined the Retribution in number and are expected to serve as the long-reaching line for the army abroad, wielding heavy rifles capable of delivering punishing firepower against the human armies that so greatly outnumber them.

Each house keeps riflemen proportionate to its means, with the remaining soldiers being troops less costly to maintain, such as halberdiers. Outfitting and maintaining rifleman companies is a considerable expense but one considered well worth it. A house boasting a sizable force of such soldiers can prove its affluence and power. Because of the cost to outfit these companies and the time invested in their training, Ios prefers quality to quantity. Every man who serves as a rifleman has spent years drilling in the use of his weapons alongside his squad. They are professional soldiers of the highest caliber. Rather than haphazardly firing into the enemy, a rifleman is trained to take careful aim and regard each trigger pull as a prospective kill.

The key to victory is discipline and coordination. We must support each other as a single body, stand firm, and fire as one. —Rifleman Captain Nyshel of House Scylassin

The stoic and keen-eyed officers who lead the houseguard rifleman companies are even more vital to their success than the individual training of the men. Victory or defeat may rest on the smallest judgment calls, like the choice of a good piece of land upon which to situate the men. These captains must be able to gauge the strength of the enemy accurately and direct the fire of their men where it is needed most. They must be sure their actions work smoothly with the convoluted plans of mage hunters and the Dawnguard. A good captain knows to hold his fire until the first mage hunter bolts strike home on unsuspecting targets. He keeps the impatience and the fears of his men in check and their focus on their targets so they will operate like a well-oiled watch.

Attachment [Houseguard Riflemen] – This attachment can be added to a unit of the type listed.

OFFICER

⊘ **Combined Ranged Attack**

⊛ **Officer**

Granted: War Tempered – While this model is in play, models in its unit can make combined ranged attacks targeting models in melee.

Ranked Attacks – Friendly Faction models can ignore this model when determining LOS.

Whites Of Their Eyes – Once per game while in formation, this model can use this ability during its unit's activation. This activation, models in this unit gain an additional die on ranged attack rolls against models within 8″ of it.

STANDARD BEARER

⊗ **Standard Bearer**

Ranked Attacks – Friendly Faction models can ignore this model when determining LOS.

OFFICER						
SPD	STR	MAT	RAT	DEF	ARM	CMD
6	4	6	6	13	13	9

LONG RIFLE			
RNG	ROF	AOE	POW
14	1	—	10

SWORD	
POW	P+S
3	7

STANDARD BEARER						
SPD	STR	MAT	RAT	DEF	ARM	CMD
6	4	5	5	13	13	8

OFFICER'S DAMAGE	5
FIELD ALLOWANCE	1
POINT COST	2
SMALL BASE	

TACTICAL TIPS

Granted: War Tempered – Do not ignore the target's DEF bonus when shooting into melee.

Officer – Because this model is an Officer, when it is destroyed it does not replace a grunt in its unit. Instead the unit leader becomes the unit commander.

After decades of directing fire, these committed career soldiers know better than anyone the pressure they can bring to bear with a few dozen rifles placed in the right place at the right time. Under such a commander riflemen stay steady in the face of incoming enemies, waiting until the last moment and thereby increasing the deadly impact of every shot.

MAGE HUNTER STRIKE FORCE
RETRIBUTION UNIT

Where others would walk meekly toward extinction, we fight to our last breath.
We will do what must be done, whatever the price. —Glyssor Syviis

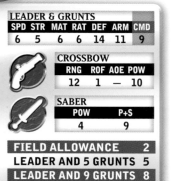

LEADER & GRUNTS						
SPD	STR	MAT	RAT	DEF	ARM	CMD
6	5	6	6	14	11	9

CROSSBOW			
RNG	ROF	AOE	POW
12	1	—	10

SABER	
POW	P+S
4	9

FIELD ALLOWANCE	2
LEADER AND 5 GRUNTS	5
LEADER AND 9 GRUNTS	8
SMALL BASE	

LEADER & GRUNTS

⊘ Combined Melee Attack

◐ Pathfinder

▤ Stealth

Arcane Assassin – When making attacks, ignore focus points overboosting the target's Power Field and spell effects adding to its ARM or DEF.

'Jack Hunter – This model gains an additional die to its melee and ranged damage rolls against warjacks.

Mage hunters constitute the traditional core of the Retribution. Mage hunter strike forces have waged a secret war against humanity for centuries. In that time the Retribution has refined its ability to recruit agents with the proper mix of dedication, raw talent, and hunter's instinct to train them into unconventional warriors and killers. Mage hunters are expected to function in circumstances regular soldiers rarely have to face, such as surviving hand-to-mouth deep in enemy territory while isolated from friendly support. They learn to be at home in any environment, to scavenge and improvise, and to kill without a moment's hesitation. Even in normal pitched battles the mage hunters use misdirection and stealth to gain the element of surprise.

Their first priority is always the elimination of enemy arcanists and mechanikal constructs—those elements believed to harm Scyrah. Borrowing on personal experience as much as knowledge passed down from their predecessors, these strike teams learn to disable mechanikal systems with practiced ease.

Initial training and drills at the Syvash Stronghold only take aspiring recruits so far, and they are not counted as full hunters until they go forth to join strike teams in one of the various operational regions in the human kingdoms. In this unforgiving environment their skills are put to the test on missions with life and death at stake. Those found lacking never last long while those who remain are hardened by field experience. In time the best of them no longer need the support of a group and can work independently.

Mage hunters belong to a fierce and zealous fellowship and are united by an unshakable belief in their cause. Not only does failure bring personal shame, but it also represents disappointing their goddess. This mind set gives each mage hunter singular focus and conviction. They know the path to Scyrah's restoration will require spilling a great deal of blood.

MAGE HUNTER STRIKE FORCE COMMANDER
RETRIBUTION UNIT ATTACHMENT

A mage hunter commander must be adept in the arts of communicating with silence, directing in darkness, and anticipating the unknowable. —Kaelyssa, Night's Whisper

Senior operatives in the organization watch the performance of veteran mage hunters closely. Those veterans who successfully lead small teams on difficult missions are evaluated and their future in the organization weighed. Though all mage hunters are prized as deadly killers, those with the instincts for leadership prove most valuable in the long run. They are promoted to command and entrusted with the lives of dozens of mage hunters or given oversight over an entire cell or base outside of Ios.

Veteran teams led by these senior commanders are well versed in advanced Retribution tactics and techniques. They plan every operation down to the last detail, utilizing surveillance and espionage to evaluate the enemy precisely. Slipping past the outer defenses of an enemy base while under cover of darkness, they fire bolts through intervening walls to kill without a trace. Those left alive in the aftermath of such attacks are often bewildered and terrified to find the bodies of their peers without any awareness of having been under attack. Working alongside other soldiers in the Retribution military, these teams apply similar methods to erase vital targets before they can even join battle.

Attachment [Mage Hunter Strike Force] – This attachment can be added to a unit of the type listed.

COMMANDER

- Combined Melee Attack
- Officer
- Pathfinder
- Stealth

Arcane Assassin – When making attacks, ignore focus points overboosting the target's Power Field and spell effects adding to its ARM or DEF.

'Jack Hunter – This model gains an additional die to its melee and ranged damage rolls against warjacks.

Tactics: Advance Deployment – Models in this unit gain Advance Deployment.

Tactics: Phantom Seeker – Models in this unit gain Phantom Seeker. (A model with Phantom Seeker ignores LOS when making ranged attacks. That model ignores concealment and cover when resolving ranged attacks.)

COMMANDER						
SPD	STR	MAT	RAT	DEF	ARM	CMD
6	5	7	7	14	11	9

CROSSBOW			
RNG	ROF	AOE	POW
12	1	—	10

SABER	
POW	P+S
4	9

DAMAGE	5
FIELD ALLOWANCE	1
POINT COST	2
SMALL BASE	

TACTICAL TIPS

Tactics: Phantom Seeker – Keep in mind that Phantom Seeker does not ignore Stealth.

Officer – Because this model is an Officer, when it is destroyed it does not replace a grunt in its unit. Instead the unit leader becomes the unit commander.

By necessity commanders operating outside Ios cannot frequently contact Retribution leadership and must be ready to act autonomously in carrying forward the goals of the sect. A commander must make good use of his subordinates, including the inevitable necessity of weighing the priorities of the mission against the survival of members of his own team.

STORMFALL ARCHERS
RETRIBUTION UNIT

Inflict on them such a torrent of thunder and fire that the enemy will not know ground from sky or night from day. —Stormfall Captain Darshyvin

LEADER & GRUNTS						
SPD	STR	MAT	RAT	DEF	ARM	CMD
5	4	5	5	13	13	8

GREAT BOW			
RNG	ROF	AOE	POW
12	1	3	12

SWORD	
POW	P+S
3	7

FIELD ALLOWANCE	2
LEADER AND 3 GRUNTS	5
SMALL BASE	

LEADER & GRUNTS

Attack Type – Each time this model makes a normal ranged attack, choose one of the following abilities:

- **Brutal Shot** – Gain an additional die on the damage roll against a model directly hit.

- **Snipe** – This attack gains +4″ RNG.

- **Star Strike** – This attack causes no damage. Instead, on a direct hit models in the AOE suffer the Fire continuous effect.

TACTICAL TIPS

Star Strike – If the attack misses, nothing happens.

Stormfall archers are walking artillery batteries that can unleash a firestorm of death and destruction from an arsenal of alchemical ammunition. Requiring only their great compound bows to launch their firepower across the battlefield, the Stormfall archers are quite unlike the slow-moving cannon crews seen in the human kingdoms. They are able to move quickly into position, open fire, and fall back before the enemy has time to respond—tactics that fit well into the Retribution's approach to war.

The Stormfall archers originated with House Rhyslyrr, but their techniques quickly spread and were adopted by many ancillary houses. While many of these archers remain among the Homeguard Coalition, a sizable number have joined other elements of the houseguard to march alongside the Retribution. Stormfall archers are more likely to be overheard discussing angles of projected descent and calculating the best attack vector rather than debating the plight of Scyrah, but this does not mean many of them lack for piety. Theirs is a highly specialized discipline, and they take great pride in the firepower they can unleash to turn the tide of battle.

Do not mourn him. By his sacrifice our men were preserved, which for one such as him at least gives his death a purpose. —Mage Hunter Commander Aleph

The parents of soulless might have a different perception of the "mercy" afforded these unwanted offspring if they knew to what use many are put. While Retribution handlers endeavor to train these unfortunates as soldiers, not every soulless is equally suitable. Some are destined to serve another function since their unique state allows them to neutralize arcane energy. Energy flows are siphoned directly into the body of the soulless, causing disfiguring burns. If he siphons too much it prompts complete organ failure. Heart and lungs burst from the hostile energy pouring into the soulless, leaving those around him untouched.

Making use of soulless in this fashion is a relatively new and experimental endeavor. For several decades sympathetic midwives and priests from the Fane of Scyrah have smuggled these unfortunate children to the Retribution. The soulless youths are then raised and trained at a sealed enclave on the outskirts of Iryss where they learn to handle weapons and obey commands. Unfortunately the absence of self-will and motivation makes many of them lackluster warriors and they may be taken aside for other tasks. One of

Attachment [Any Retribution Unit] – This attachment can be added to a unit of the type listed.

ESCORT

Disbinding (★Action) – Enemy upkeep spells on this model and/or its unit immediately expire.

Flank [Another model in this unit] – When this model makes a melee attack against an enemy model within the melee range of a friendly model of the listed type, this model gains +2 to attack rolls and gains an additional damage die.

Mage Static – While this model is in formation, enemy magic attacks targeting a model in this model's unit suffer –5 RNG.

Soulless – This model does not generate a soul token when it is destroyed.

Tag Along – This model does not gain the abilities of the unit to which it is attached except Advance Deployment.

SWORD

⊘ **Magical Weapon**

ESCORT						
SPD	STR	MAT	RAT	DEF	ARM	CMD
6	6	5	3	13	12	10

SWORD		
	POW	P+S
	3	9

FIELD ALLOWANCE	3
1 ESCORT	1
UP TO 2 ADDITIONAL ESCORTS	1 EA
SMALL BASE	

TACTICAL TIPS

Tag Along – Tactics is one of the unit abilities this model doesn't gain.

Yes, they can be attached to any Retribution unit.

the favored uses of these individuals is to exploit their ability to interfere with enemy arcane energies. They serve almost as lightning rods to preserve the lives of others in the Retribution from hostile magic.

The units to whom these escorts are attached do not take well to a soulless in their midst. The escort is never considered a true part of the group. Some are treated like pack animals and never spoken to at all.

ARCANIST
RETRIBUTION SOLO

Each myrmidon has a soul of its own, arising from the smoothly running harmony of every piece and transcending the sum of its components. —Arcanist Myrvenn to his new apprentice

ARCANIST						
SPD	STR	MAT	RAT	DEF	ARM	CMD
6	5	5	4	13	12	8

MULTI TOOL		
	POW	P+S
	3	8

FIELD ALLOWANCE	2
POINT COST	1
SMALL BASE	

ARCANIST

Concentrated Power (★Action) – RNG 5. Target friendly Faction warjack. If the warjack is in range, it gains +2 on melee damage rolls this turn.

Power Booster (★Action) – RNG 5. Target friendly Faction warjack. If the target warjack is in range and has no focus points, it gains 1 focus point. If the warjack is Disrupted, it is no longer Disrupted.

Repair [8] (★Action) – This model can attempt repairs on any damaged friendly Faction warjack. To attempt repairs, this model must be B2B with the damaged warjack and make a skill check. If successful, remove d6 damage points from the warjack's damage grid.

producing myrmidons has its own techniques, standards, and secrets. Maintaining such machines requires highly specialized skills passed down from master to apprentice. Every arcanist is answerable to his mentor or another house agent tasked to ensure the confidentiality of Shyeel secrets. They work amid the grease and oil of machinery, far removed from house politics, and they are rarely distracted by matters of religion.

TACTICAL TIPS

Repair – A wreck marker cannot be repaired.

Even the most masterfully crafted myrmidon requires repair and support, particularly after the rigors of battle. Energy condensers and field projectors are rugged pieces of military hardware, but direct hits that breach the power field will inevitably damage more delicate internal elements. Arcanists are seasoned mechanics with a broad working knowledge of arcanika that allows them to piece together shattered and broken hardware to get even a mostly ruined myrmidon working again. Their expertise allows them to lend subtle arcane power to push these machines to the limit.

Arcanists require a degree of bravery and grit to maintain their focus in the chaos of battle while myrmidons under their charge are hammered with shells or pummeled by hammers and axes. Arcanists have a more intimate working knowledge of how myrmidons actually function than anyone. Those who design these machines in the sheltered confines of House Shyeel never have to rush to figure out how to pry open a dented access panel and replace a shattered focusing lens before enemy rifles close to firing range.

Most arcanists in the employ of the Retribution are affiliated with House Shyeel, belonging either to the house directly or to one of several affiliate houses of lower standing. Each of the few houses capable of

DAWNGUARD DESTOR THANE
RETRIBUTION CAVALRY SOLO

Once we commit to this action there can be no hesitation or withdrawal. We will crush the enemy under our hooves or we will fall. —Destor Thane Hylvas Nyarr

Each destor thane is a stalwart veteran of the Dawnguard mounted tradition. They are grim-faced ranking officers entrusted to oversee the perfect execution of battle plans involving multiple captains and their respective companies. These mounted warriors take considerable pride in their reputations as being an army in one. After years fighting in the saddle they are singularly skilled with their lance cannons, able to fire multiple blasts in sequence or charge to obliterate their enemies with the weight of their armored steeds.

In the civil war against House Vyre these expert cavalry leaders made the difference in breaking through defenders outside Iryss, and many of those veterans have gone on to become prominent leaders among the Dawnguard. Warcasters rely heavily upon the thanes not only for their martial prowess but also for their proven leadership and unique perspective of the battlefield.

THANE

⭐ **Commander**

🌀 **Gunfighter**

Unyielding – While engaging an enemy model, this model gains +2 ARM.

Virtuoso – This model can make melee and ranged attacks during the same combat action. When this model makes its initial attacks, it can make both its initial ranged and melee attacks.

LANCE CANNON

Multi-Fire (★Attack) – Make an attack with this weapon. On a hit, after resolving the attack this model can immediately make one additional attack with this weapon targeting the last model hit or another model within 2″ of the last model hit, ignoring ROF. This model can make up to four attacks during its activation as a result of Multi-Fire.

LANCE

Lance – This weapon can be used only to make charge attacks. When this model charges, this weapon gains reach until the charge is resolved.

THANE						
SPD	STR	MAT	RAT	DEF	ARM	CMD
8	7	8	7	13	17	10

LANCE CANNON			
RNG	ROF	AOE	POW
10	1	—	12

LANCE	
POW	P+S
7	14

MOUNT
POW
10

DAMAGE	10
FIELD ALLOWANCE	2
POINT COST	4
LARGE BASE	

Many officers among the destors believe the true potential of heavy cavalry has yet to be realized. Not content merely to support infantry offensives, these officers await the chance to prove their value on battlefields far from the confines of Ios. For years the only true threat to an Iosan army has come from within. Now is the opportunity for innovative officers to prove their mettle against unpredictable and unknown threats. These thanes embrace the opportunities for battle afforded them by the Retribution, and they are eager to test their theories against the chaos of true war.

TACTICAL TIPS

Multi-Fire – Multi-Fire ignores ROF but does not ignore RNG. Additional attacks against targets beyond this weapon's range will automatically miss. This model cannot make a Multi-Fire special attack if it charges.

DAWNGUARD SCYIR
RETRIBUTION SOLO

Rank is not a reward. It is a punishment inflicted on those too diligent and ambitious to know they would be happier without the added burden. —Garryth, Blade of Retribution

SCYIR						
SPD	STR	MAT	RAT	DEF	ARM	CMD
6	6	8	4	13	15	10

GREAT SWORD		
	POW	P+S
	6	12

DAMAGE	5
FIELD ALLOWANCE	2
POINT COST	2
SMALL BASE	

SCYIR

⭐ **Commander**

✴ **'Jack Marshal**

Coordinated Strike – This model and myrmidons it controls can ignore friendly Dawnguard models when drawing LOS and can advance through friendly Dawnguard models if they have enough movement to move completely past the Dawnguard models' bases.

Drive: Reroll – This model can attempt to Drive each warjack under its control in its command range. To Drive a warjack, this model must make a command check at any time during its activation. If the check succeeds, the warjack can reroll one missed attack roll during its activation this turn.

Flank [Faction Warjack] – When this model makes a melee attack against an enemy model within the melee range of a friendly model of the listed type, this model gains +2 to attack rolls and gains an additional damage die.

Iron Sentinel – While B2B with a friendly Faction warjack, this model gains +2 DEF and ARM and cannot be knocked down.

GREAT SWORD

⊘ **Reach**

Scyirs are rightfully considered lords of the battlefield, and each is widely recognized for his individual deeds. Not only are they personally formidable, but scyirs must also simultaneously direct both myrmidons and all branches of the Dawnguard. In the absence of a warcaster they are often given a similar degree of operational oversight. Indeed, in the recent past scyirs enjoyed unquestioned authority and autonomy over their subordinates once battle began.

That role has shifted since House Nyarr joined the Retribution. Scyirs must deal with the added complications of coordinating efforts alongside mage hunter commanders and similarly ranked members of the houseguard. The scyirs who will succeed in the Retribution will be those who can earn the genuine respect of their peers rather than expecting unquestioning obedience.

Scyirs are the first of several elevated ranks in the Iosan military tradition, those at the highest echelons who borrow their titles from the Divine Court. To be worthy of this stature, scyirs must prove themselves as the elite of the elite. Ranking above captains and thanes, scyirs may be tasked to lead task forces of mixed forces. Most are sons and daughters of nobility. For those concentrating on the battlefield rather than politics there is no need to aspire to higher rank. These knights represent the pinnacle of Dawnguard martial coordination and are allowed to focus all their energy on these tasks and avoid the petty distractions of logistics and politics that occupy their superiors.

HOUSE SHYEEL MAGISTER
RETRIBUTION BATTLE MAGE SOLO

Those with the will can shape the world rather than being shaped by it. —House Shyeel Magister Larshiv

Battle mage magisters demonstrate even greater control over the evocation of raw force than their subordinates as they walk unconcerned into oncoming mortar and rifle fire. With a simple exertion of mental strength they manipulate invisible energies to tear an enemy limb from limb or to haul massive machinery around like pieces on a game board. Those seeking to close to engage them directly are often surprised to discover that the massive arcanika gauntlets they wear serve not only as conduits for their powers but also as formidable weapons in their own right. These fists can deliver tremendous crushing blows and send opponents flying.

Magisters are unforgiving of failure and impatient with those they consider their mental inferiors. Even among their allies they are treated like forces of nature that must be appeased and entreated and are capable of unleashing unimaginable destructive power. They do not readily submit to orders from outsiders. Even ranking Dawnguard

MAGISTER

Force Barrier – This model gains +2 DEF against ranged attack rolls and does not suffer blast damage.

MAGIC ABILITY [7]

- **Force Bolt (★Attack)** – Force Bolt is a RNG 10, POW 10 magic attack. An enemy model hit by this attack can be pushed d3˝ directly toward or away from this model. Choose the direction before rolling the distance. On a critical hit, the enemy model is knocked down after being pushed.

- **Whip Snap (★Attack)** – Whip Snap is a RNG 6, POW 12 magic attack. If this attack hits an enemy model, immediately after the attack is resolved this model or a friendly model within 3˝ of it can advance up to 3˝. A friendly model can advance as a result of this spell only once per turn.

POWER GAUNTLETS

⊘ **Magical Weapon**

Beat Back – Immediately after a normal attack with this weapon is resolved during this model's combat action, the enemy model hit can be pushed 1˝ directly away from the attacking model. After the enemy model is pushed, the attacking model can advance up to 1˝.

Combo Smite (★Attack) – Make a melee attack. On a hit, instead of making a normal damage roll, the target model is slammed d6˝ directly away from this model and suffers a damage roll with POW equal to the STR of this model plus twice the POW of this weapon. The POW of collateral damage is equal to this model's STR.

MAGISTER						
SPD	STR	MAT	RAT	DEF	ARM	CMD
6	7	7	4	13	12	9

POWER GAUNTLET		
×2	POW	P+S
	4	11

DAMAGE	5
FIELD ALLOWANCE	2
POINT COST	2
SMALL BASE	

officers and mage hunter commanders are inclined to request rather than demand their cooperation. Magisters often convey secret instructions and contingencies from house leaders, and thus they have influence even beyond their apparent rank. Retribution officers who antagonize the magisters may find myrmidons and support staff in short supply. They might also receive a personal visit from these formidable mages demanding redress for their disrespect.

TACTICAL TIPS

Beat Back – The attacking model can advance even if the enemy model is destroyed by the attack.

Combo Smite – Remember, the slammed model is moved only half the distance rolled if it has a larger base than the slamming model.

MAGE HUNTER ASSASSIN
RETRIBUTION SOLO

The taking of life is a holy rite whereby a soul is returned to its maker. It is right to fear those who are eminently skilled in this task. —Lyliss, Nis-Scyir of Autumn and Court Assassin

ASSASSIN						
SPD	STR	MAT	RAT	DEF	ARM	CMD
7	5	7	4	15	12	9

CHAIN BLADE		
	POW	P+S
	4	9

DAMAGE	5
FIELDS ALLOWANCE	2
POINT COST	2
SMALL BASE	

ASSASSIN

- Advance Deployment
- Pathfinder
- Stealth

Arcane Assassin – When making attacks, ignore focus points overboosting the target's Power Field and spell effects adding to its ARM or DEF.

CHAIN BLADE

- Weapon Master

Chain Strike – This weapon has a 4″ melee range during this model's activation.

Chain Weapon – This attack ignores the Buckler and Shield advantages and Shield Wall.

Decapitation – Damage exceeding the ARM of the model hit is doubled. A model disabled by this attack cannot make a Tough roll.

This cult vanished along with the city of Shaelvas, but its practices were carried on by a few, and they eventually joined the Retribution and dedicated their lives to avenging Scyrah. They became a small and specialized offshoot of the mage hunters who maintain their unique martial traditions. As a group they are insular and take pride in their unique and deadly skills. Recruitment for this cabal is slow, for their chain blades are tricky to master and require exceptional reflexes. A skilled assassin can send the blade flying tremendous distances before whipping the chain to bring the weapon to hand, ready for close-quarter fighting.

Mage hunter assassins are practiced killers with the refined skills to pose a threat to anyone unfortunate enough to be selected as their target. Advancing in silence, these fanatics can bring down even the mighty warcasters with deadly and far-reaching strikes. If a mage hunter assassin successful closes with her enemy, chances are that the target is as good as dead.

The Retribution seems to be a cohesive sect, but it is really the amalgam of several ancient cults brought together in the early years after its founding. Among these groups was a cult of warrior-monks who mastered a fighting form called *klyvenesh*, or "the striking serpent." This cult served as secretive guardians of the Fane of Lyliss, the goddess of autumn. The Consulate Court made infrequent use of these assassins to eliminate those deemed a threat to the government.

There is nothing so sublime as the absolute silence following the report of my rifle as I watch through the scope as my target falls to the ground. —Ghost Sniper Gryion Mashyvel

Ghost snipers are specialized and secretive hunter-killers employed ostensibly to help patrol the borders by bringing their powerful rifles to bear against intruders. They have an ominous reputation among both Homeguard Coalition officers and the ordinary citizenry. Rumors persist that these cold killers are sometimes engaged to eliminate Iosans who are deemed potentially dangerous. Many nobles would be horrified to learn that a sizable number of snipers have joined the Retribution.

Ghosts do not function as a single cohesive organization but rather as a group of individuals focused on the same skills and tasks. Snipers of proven skill among lower houses take

GHOST SNIPER

⊙ **Pathfinder**

🕭 **Stealth**

Camouflage – This model gains an additional +2 DEF when benefiting from concealment or cover.

Swift Hunter – When this model destroys an enemy model with a normal ranged attack, immediately after the attack is resolved it can advance up to 2˝.

ARCANE CANNON

Deadly Shot (★Attack) – Instead of rolling damage, a model hit suffers 3 damage points. When damaging a warjack or warbeast, choose which column or branch suffers the damage.

GHOST SNIPER						
SPD	STR	MAT	RAT	DEF	ARM	CMD
6	4	4	7	14	11	8

ARCANE CANNON			
RNG	ROF	AOE	POW
14	1	—	10

SWORD	
POW	P+S
3	7

DAMAGE	5
FIELD ALLOWANCE	2
POINT COST	2
SMALL BASE	

TACTICAL TIPS

Camouflage – If a model ignores concealment or cover, it also ignores Camouflage.

on this pseudo-military role to offer their services to officers and nobles of the Five Great Military Houses. While it has never been openly discussed, any of these nobles can call on ghosts for escort protection and have limited rights to assign them tasks. It is not uncommon for ghost snipers to supplement regular military forces as added fire support and protection, sometimes without the soldiers being aware of their presence.

When Houses Nyarr and Shyeel allied with the Retribution and began mustering the houseguard, a number of ghost snipers offered their services as well. Many were already sympathetic to the Retribution while others simply sought profit and a chance to exercise their skills abroad. Whatever their reasons, these killers have chosen to sight their formidable rifles at the enemies of the Retribution.

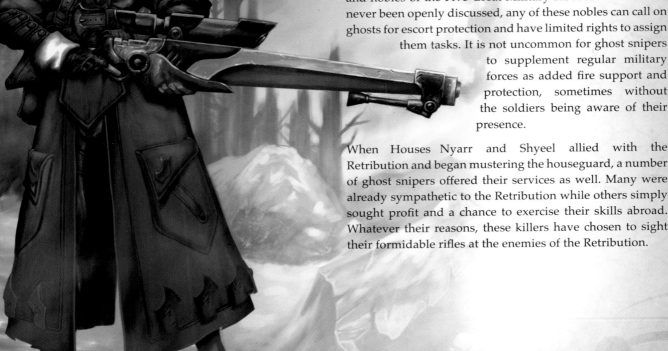

EIRYSS, MAGE HUNTER OF IOS
MERCENARY CHARACTER SOLO

Though I do not question her effectiveness, I share no enthusiasm for her work. How she restrains herself from cutting their throats, I cannot fathom. —Garryth, Blade of Retribution

EIRYSS						
SPD	STR	MAT	RAT	DEF	ARM	CMD
7	4	6	9	16	12	9

CROSSBOW			
RNG	ROF	AOE	POW
12	1	—	10

BAYONET	
POW	P+S
2	6

SABER	
POW	P+S
3	7

DAMAGE	5
FIELD ALLOWANCE	C
POINT COST	3
SMALL BASE	

Mercenary – This model will work for Cygnar, Khador, the Protectorate, and the Retribution.

EIRYSS

⊙ **Advance Deployment**

✹ **Fearless**

⚘ **Pathfinder**

⚑ **Stealth**

Attack Type – Each time this model makes a normal ranged attack, choose one of the following abilities:

- **Death Bolt** – Instead of rolling damage, a model hit suffers 3 damage points. When damaging a warjack or warbeast, choose which column or branch suffers the damage.

- **Disruptor Bolt** – A model hit loses all focus points. A model hit with the Focus Manipulation special rule does not replenish focus points next turn. A warjack hit suffers Disruption for one round. (A warjack suffering Disruption loses its focus points and cannot be allocated focus or channel spells for one round.)

- **Phantom Seeker** – This model ignores LOS when making ranged attacks. This model ignores concealment and cover when resolving ranged attacks.

Camouflage — This model gains an additional +2 DEF when benefiting from concealment or cover.

Retribution Partisan – When included in a Retribution army, this model is a Retribution model.

Technological Intolerance – When this model ends its normal movement within 5˝ of a friendly non-myrmidon warjack, its activation ends immediately.

TACTICAL TIPS

Disruptor Bolt – Just as with Disruption, Disruptor Bolt does not prevent a model from gaining focus in other ways. A warcaster can still gain focus from soul tokens, for example.

Phantom Seeker – Keep in mind that Phantom Seeker does not ignore Stealth.

Camouflage – If a model ignores concealment or cover, it also ignores Camouflage.

Keldeacon Synvas Uithuyr, the Retribution's training master, first recognized Eiryss as a person of unusual talent. He saw in her not only formidable martial prowess, but more importantly a singular will. She proved the veracity of this assessment when she was sent to join a covert cell operating outside Ios. She quickly outpaced the other members of her team, achieving mission objectives alone or despite the blunders of peers. In time she attracted the attention of Narn, who took her under his charge and guided her transformation into an assassin. She proved to be a worthy disciple and went on to belong among the foremost Retribution agents.

After several years at such work Eiryss found the limits of traditional operational procedures. Retribution techniques were effective at killing individuals, particularly civilian wizards, but they failed elsewhere. While the Retribution had gained a comprehensive awareness of the broad capabilities of the human kingdom militaries, they had limited access to information regarding the allocation of specific high-priority assets such as powerful arcanists and warcasters. These targets proved to be the most elusive and tenacious. There was only so much mage hunters could learn from the outside, and as Iosans they could never infiltrate these organizations as members.

Eiryss is unusual not for the kills she has accumulated, although there are many, nor for her skill, which is considerable, but rather for her unconventional methods. Most Retribution operatives could never stomach even brief interactions with their enemy outside of what might be required to extract information. For decades Eiryss has adopted the guise of a mercenary, selling her services to those she has sworn to kill. This coldly calculating game of winning trust and betraying her employers has prompted both respect and incomprehension from her peers within the Retribution.

Eiryss committed herself to a radically different approach to intelligence gathering, developing her signature methodology of hiring her services to the enemy in order to learn their secrets. Proof of this technique's effectiveness molders in graves across the Iron Kingdoms. Even the Nine Voices of the Retribution have been amazed at her ongoing success, as Eiryss has proven her genius by accomplishing these repeated assassinations without alienating her clients. Over the years she has walked this tightrope constantly, selling her services to one army after another in order to gain the chance to kill enemy wizards as well as to learn about those who hire her. It is a largely solitary existence, although Eiryss has remained in contact with Retribution cells abroad, through which she provides information regarding the movements of the enemy.

The vital intelligence she has sent via these channels to Retribution commanders operating in Ios and abroad has allowed them to conduct operations that would otherwise have had no chance of success. Eiryss has carefully managed her activities to divert suspicion of her former employers even as they were struck down by the Retribution. Both Khador and Cygnar in particular are accustomed to dealing fast and loose with mercenaries and often neglect detailed records of such arrangements, a fact Eiryss uses to her advantage.

Eiryss has helped unearth a wealth of information on warcasters and other ranking officers in the human armies. With this, the Retribution of Scyrah has created a comprehensive portrait of the armies of their enemies, and they intend to use this information liberally in days to come. Meanwhile Eiryss still moves freely among her enemy, a hidden viper awaiting her moment to strike.

EIRYSS, ANGEL OF RETRIBUTION
MERCENARY EPIC MAGE HUNTER CHARACTER SOLO

*We are the blades of retribution. The time has come to mete punishments so terrible
the gods themselves will weep for our enemies.* —Eiryss

EIRYSS						
SPD	STR	MAT	RAT	DEF	ARM	CMD
7	4	6	9	16	12	9

CROSSBOW			
RNG	ROF	AOE	POW
12	1	—	10

SABER	
POW	P+S
3	7

BAYONET	
POW	P+S
2	6

DAMAGE	5
FIELD ALLOWANCE	C
POINT COST	3
SMALL BASE	

Mercenary – This model will work for Cygnar, Khador, the Protectorate, and the Retribution.

EIRYSS

- ⬇ **Advance Deployment**
- ✠ **Fearless**
- ☾ **Pathfinder**
- ⚑ **Stealth**

Arcane Interference – When this model hits another model with an attack, upkeep spells and animi on the model hit expire and it loses the focus points on it. When this model hits a warjack with an attack, that warjack suffers Disruption. (A warjack suffering Disruption loses its focus points and cannot be allocated focus or channel spells for one round.)

Camouflage – This model gains an additional +2 DEF when benefiting from concealment or cover.

Retribution Partisan – When included in a Retribution army, this model is a Retribution model instead of a Mercenary model.

Sniper – When damaging a warjack or warbeast with a ranged attack, choose which column or branch suffers damage. Instead of rolling damage on a ranged attack, this model can inflict 1 damage point. A model that participates in a combined ranged attack loses Sniper until the attack is resolved.

Technological Interference – While within 5˝ of this model, non-myrmidon warjacks cannot channel spells or be allocated focus.

Whiplash – When an enemy model misses this model with a magic attack, the attacking model becomes the target and is automatically hit by the attack. AOE magic attacks that miss are centered on the attacking model. This model is the point of origin for all these attacks.

For years Eiryss has swallowed her hatred of humanity and hunted spellcasters on the battlegrounds of mankind, and many who profane Caen with foul sorceries have fallen to her bolts and blade. While her methods have never been entirely embraced by her peers, her fellow mage hunters nonetheless see Eiryss as an anointed angel of wrath who embodies everything the Retribution strives to achieve.

She became something more after the pivotal events in Korsk when she confirmed the survival of Nyssor. Swept

TACTICAL TIPS

Camouflage – If a model ignores concealment or cover, it also ignores Camouflage.

up in events that culminated in a direct confrontation with Goreshade, the eldritch who had once been Ghyrrshyld, Eiryss came upon the unholy creature's attempt at deicide. This drove her to such rage that she pursued him as he fled. In retrospect, Eiryss considers her actions reckless—and Goreshade a fool for leaving her wounded but alive. The creature had felt compelled to explain his actions in a vain attempt to convince her they shared a similar purpose. In doing so he had revealed his deranged plan to murder not just Nyssor but Scyrah as well, as part of a mad scheme to restore Ios' spiritual balance.

Eiryss ignored her wounds to return to the scene of Goreshade's blasphemy and witnessed Nyssor's frozen vault being stolen by Khadoran Greylords. Too injured to continue the pursuit, she proved her worth by returning to Ios to relate a tale that would shock and electrify citizens across the elven nation and stir the Retribution to full war readiness.

Eiryss sees herself as simply another soldier in the cause and believes she did only what had to be done. Despite this pragmatic attitude, she has served as a rallying point for the Retribution. Particularly among the younger and more idealistic recruits, the legend of Eiryss has assumed almost mythic proportions.

Eiryss ignores this adoration to focus on her ongoing crusade. She fights for Scyrah and proclaims her hatred of humanity with every deadly bolt fired from her crossbow. The intricate dance she conducts of hiring her services to her enemies has reached a new and more dangerous peak. The Retribution's march to war only escalates her risk, and she is convinced she lives now on borrowed time. This only pushes her to work harder to pave the way for the success of those who will follow her. So long as Goreshade plots the death of the Iosan gods, so long as human wizards despoil their divine power, Eiryss cannot rest.

Her role abroad remains as vital as before. She has been urged by Retribution leaders to resume her work and even to increase her contact with warcasters serving in the human armies. The intelligence she can discover in this capacity is impossible to replicate by other means and should give the Retribution a powerful edge in the conflicts ahead.

FANE KNIGHT SKERYTH ISSYEN
RETRIBUTION DRAGOON CHARACTER SOLO

That one is uncorrupted. I fear for what may become of his soul, but we require his strength. —Ravyn, the Eternal Light

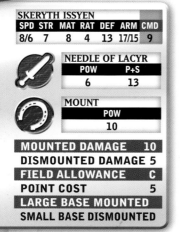

SKERYTH ISSYEN						
SPD	STR	MAT	RAT	DEF	ARM	CMD
8/6	7	8	4	13	17/15	9

NEEDLE OF LACYR	
POW	P+S
6	13

MOUNT
POW
10

MOUNTED DAMAGE	10
DISMOUNTED DAMAGE	5
FIELD ALLOWANCE	C
POINT COST	5
LARGE BASE MOUNTED	
SMALL BASE DISMOUNTED	

SKERYTH ISSYEN

Dragoon – While mounted, this model has base SPD 8 and base ARM 17. While dismounted, it has base SPD 6, base ARM 15.

Rapid Strike – This model can make one additional melee attack each combat action.

Righteous Fury – When one or more friendly Faction warrior models are destroyed by an enemy attack while in this model's command range, this model gains +2 STR and ARM for one round.

NEEDLE OF LACYR

Ⓜ **Magical Weapon**

Ⓡ **Reach**

Ⓦ **Weapon Master**

Blessed – When making an attack with this weapon, ignore spell effects that add to a model's ARM or DEF.

Fane Knights are soldiers who have answered a divine calling and feel chosen to pledge their lives to the defense of Scyrah. They have vowed to protect both the fane and the goddess to their last heartbeat. Standing guard in the immediate presence of Scyrah, Skeryth Issyen looked upon her perfect divine beauty with his own eyes and each day felt agony over his powerlessness. Despite the warnings of his priests and superiors, he has turned to the Retribution for answers.

Though he is a blood noble of one of the Five Great Military Houses of Ios, Skeryth forsook all family ties to join the Fane Knights. The reasons for his estrangement from House Issyen are not widely known but are rooted in secrets dating back to the War of the Houses, when he was still a youth.

During those difficult times he learned that the lords of his house were involved in reprehensible agreements and concessions. Back room deals were made with House Vyre that guaranteed House Issyen its position regardless of the outcome of the civil war. In return Issyen agreed to withhold its resources and stand apart from the conflict, remaining neutral throughout the war. Skeryth left his house as soon

as he learned of the deeper depravities conducted by High Consul Ghyrrshyld of Vyre. He has not publicly spoken out against his house, perhaps from some small, retained sense of family obligation, but he immediately sought membership with the knighthood sworn to serve the Fane of Scyrah. Despite his youth, he proved himself worthy by succeeding in their rigorous trials of initiation.

Skeryth found a new home among his brothers and sisters of the Fane Knights. He has spent the majority of the last two and a half decades serving the fane, first in Iryss and later in Shyrr. Three years ago Skeryth was invited to stand vigil over the goddess in her chambers, the highest honor a fane knight may hope to achieve.

The longer Skeryth spent in the Presence, the deeper grew his frustration at the need for his duty. He began to realize the futility of his vigil and feel compelled to find more active means to serve Scyrah. For this reason he was quite receptive when Ravyn, the Eternal Light of the Retribution, approached him with the request to join their cause. Skeryth had briefly served under Ravyn before she had abandoned the Fane Knights, and her persuasive arguments resonated with his own doubts.

Not willing to abandon his order entirely, Skeryth remains a Fane Knight. There are those among the priesthood who believed his presence near Retribution forces would be an advantage to the fane in days to come, and he convinced his superiors to allow him to march alongside the Retribution as an observer. His peers do not understand why he would surrender such a precious and privileged post to choose this path, but they have not stood in his way.

Skeryth has no intention of simply observing. He longs for battle and increasingly rests his hopes on the Retribution's claim that fighting humanity will provide relief to the goddess. Having come to believe that humanity is certainly at fault for Scyrah's woes, Skeryth at last has a tangible enemy against whom he can direct his wrath. In this regard, the Retribution has rekindled a hope he had thought lost. Skeryth knows he may never see Scyrah again but accepts this sacrifice in the hope that venturing abroad will let him help restore her health. Should that prove impossible, he intends to exact a terrible vengeance on those responsible for her decline.

While Skeryth's life has been spent preparing for battle, he has never seen war's horrors firsthand. Whether he will be capable of true ruthlessness against the Retribution's enemies has yet to be proven. The years ahead will likely be a trial for the fane knight, challenging both his piety and his personal notions of honor. Indeed, war may take him on a dark path away from the solemn grace of the goddess for whom he undertakes it.

NAYL
RETRIBUTION MAGE HUNTER SOULLESS CHARACTER SOLO

Do not be fooled. Despite the illusion of life, he exists only to kill and die for our cause. —Keldeacon Synvas Uithuyr

NAYL						
SPD	STR	MAT	RAT	DEF	ARM	CMD
7	7	7	3	13	12	10

TWO-HANDED SWORD		
	POW	P+S
	6	13

DAMAGE	5
FIELD ALLOWANCE	C
POINT COST	2
SMALL BASE	

NAYL

⊕ **Advance Deployment**

✵ **Fearless**

⬢ **Stealth**

Arcane Annihilation – When this model is destroyed by an enemy attack, models within 8˝ of it lose their focus and fury points and cannot cast spells, channel, or use their animi for one round.

Soulless – This model does not generate a soul token when it is destroyed.

Spell Ward – This model cannot be targeted by spells.

TWO-HANDED SWORD

⊘ **Magical Weapon**

⊙ **Reach**

TACTICAL TIPS

Spell Ward – This model is shielded from friendly and enemy spells alike.

Nayl is a walking paradox, an Iosan who might have been killed at birth and who lives only by the intervention of the Retribution of Scyrah. He is destined to stand forever apart from his people, an uncomfortable reminder of the doom awaiting Scyrah and all of Ios. In due time his life will be expended without regret and none will mourn his death. None of these truths bother him, for Nayl is one of the soulless. Such emotions as self-doubt or loneliness are as alien to him as happiness, anger, or desire. He knows nothing about his birth parents, and his only family has been his Retribution handlers and task force commanders.

His mind suffers the same eerie calm as those of the rest of the soulless. While addressing others he stares at them coolly with unmistakable black eyes, his voice devoid of substantial inflection. On the occasions he tries to mimic normal facial expressions, it is more unsettling than helpful—his mockery of a smile does not touch the void of his eyes. His posture and every gesture are calculated, rehearsed. Despite these things, Nayl is an individual. He demonstrates cunning, a certain curiosity about the world, and an understated need to please his superiors. These combine to create the shadow of a personality, albeit recognizable as such only to those who have had lengthy exposure to his kind.

The aspects of a soulless that make them useful can also inhibit their development. They follow orders precisely, for example, but this literal adherence to instruction imposes difficulties in battle, which often requires adaptability. Retribution commanders have struggled with this dilemma for decades. Nayl represents a particular success in this regard, one his trainers have had difficulty repeating. He has demonstrated an ability to learn and adapt that is often lacking in those of his kind. From the first day he lifted a blade, his trainers observed an emerging enthusiasm. Standing at rest Nayl seems blank and empty, yet a blade in his hand moves almost with a will of its own, as though expressing echoes of emotions. He communicates better by slash, thrust, and killing strike than by words.

Nayl has been honed to be a living weapon from the time his potential was first recognized. He takes no apparent pride in his work and kills as instructed without registering any sense of accomplishment. Nonetheless some deeper drive compels him to labor to improve his skill between missions. He spends hours in silent practice and constantly seeks out sparring partners among mage hunters who inevitably tire and withdraw before Nayl shows any signs of fatigue.

Exploiting qualities in the soulless that interfere with the flow of magic, Nayl's trainers prepared him from the beginning to serve as an arcane vortex. He has undergone extensive mental conditioning to ensure that his death in combat will produce an irresistible vacuum of arcane power. It was generally expected he would have served this role and perished years ago, and it is a testament to his skills that he has endured so many years and has yet to fulfill this ultimate function. Recognizing his talent, his commanders now intend to make considerable use of him as a killing machine before letting him perform this last sacrifice.

The legendary mage hunter and warcaster Garryth, Blade of Retribution, has frequently utilized Nayl in operations abroad. This preference for the soulless' companionship does not indicate friendship between the two but simply reflects Garryth's tolerance for Nayl's company over that of his peers.

Nayl completes every task with reliable and deadly efficiency, each day awaiting the order that will end his life. Meanwhile he obeys the complex codes of behavior instilled in him since childhood by the Retribution of Scyrah, codes by which he leads what passes for a life among soulless. He protects his fellow Iosans and ends the lives of their enemies, showing no preference for one of these tasks over the other.

NARN, MAGE HUNTER OF IOS
RETRIBUTION CHARACTER SOLO

Narn achieves with his blades what would, in nature, require a plague. —Glyssor Syviis, one of the Nine Voices of the Retribution

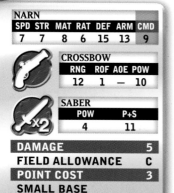

NARN						
SPD	STR	MAT	RAT	DEF	ARM	CMD
7	7	8	6	15	13	9

CROSSBOW			
RNG	ROF	AOE	POW
12	1	—	10

SABER	
POW	P+S
4	11

DAMAGE	5
FIELD ALLOWANCE	C
POINT COST	3
SMALL BASE	

NARN
◉ **Advance Deployment**
✖ **Fearless**
◐ **Pathfinder**
▯ **Stealth**

Acrobatics – This model can advance through other models if it has enough movement to move completely past their bases. This model cannot be targeted by free strikes. This model ignores intervening models when declaring its charge target.

Arcane Assassin – When making attacks, ignore focus points overboosting the target's Power Field and spell effects adding to its ARM or DEF.

Sprint – At the end of this model's activation, if it destroyed one or more enemy models with melee attacks this activation it can make a full advance.

SABER
◉ **Weapon Master**

While his name is largely unknown outside the Retribution, within their ranks Narn is held in legendary esteem for his blinding speed as a bladesman and the fluid yet austere grace by which he executes every kill. As one of the eldest active mage hunters, he has single-handedly eliminated more targets than any other agent except possibly Eiryss, his foremost protégé and greatest disciple. Indeed the most lasting testament to Narn's life's work is the fact that for a hundred years he has had a hand in training many of the sect's foremost mage hunters.

Narn has never taught at Syvash Stronghold, however. He does not consider himself an instructor, and he has no patience for the uninitiated. Rather he has often become a mentor to those mage hunters who have already demonstrated exceptional prowess. Once these aspiring assassins reach the limit of their capabilities Narn steps in to shatter any habits he considers detrimental and to mold them, sometimes by ruthlessly harsh methods, into more efficient killers.

The veteran hunter is given tremendous flexibility in his choice of operations and favors serving as a lone assassin rather than as a task force leader. Although he is adept at commanding others, he prefers to plan his own operations without direct oversight. No Retribution commander would refuse his aid, and his arrival on a given battlefield is heralded as both a welcome and an ominous event. When Narn chooses to participate in broader Retribution operations it is often a sign of the dire importance of the task at hand. He has an uncanny knack of arriving precisely where he is most needed, often transforming what would have been a botched kill into a success.

Narn has traveled throughout the Iron Kingdoms but prefers to operate in northern Cygnar, Llael, and close to the Iosan border. A number of Greylords in occupied Llael have met their end by his blades in recent months, as have members of the Llaelese Resistance. He has clearly taken an interest in the goals of Winter's Hammer and has been assisting in the planned recovery of Nyssor.

Even those who have apprenticed under him describe Narn as quiet and elusive. He speaks as little as possible and prefers to communicate by accenting his few words with gestures and small shifts in expression. His piercing eyes betray no hint of his inner thoughts, and if his reflexes have dulled with the weight of age, only he is capable of perceiving the difference. He is a killer who can spring to full attack from a resting position with no warning, wielding his blades with such skill that he gives his enemy no chance to evade death.

Eiryss is one of the few individuals with whom Narn shares any of his thoughts, and she has never been one to divulge them to others. Both lone hunters by nature, the two are sometimes seen working together in comfortable mutual silence, as regal and deadly as a pair of hawks on the wing.

The Retribution of Scyrah offers many unique oppurtunities for any aspiring miniatures painter. The shapes that compose their armor and clothing as well as the muted colors that comprise their color scheme pose many unexpected challenges. To help painters recreate our studio paint scheme, we have assembled a comprehensive overview of how we painted our Retribution figures. In the following pages you'll find all you need to know, from how to paint the shiny metallic weapons to techniques for painting the white armor plates. We even cover methods for creating eye-catching hair color. Let's get started painting some elves!

IOSAN FLESH

The elves of Ios have very pale and sallow flesh. This emphasizes their arrogant and vengeful nature and serves to set them apart from the human races. Do not worry if the face looks pink after the first shade layer because you will balance the color with a warm green shade later.

1
Basecoat the flesh with an equal mixture of Ryn Flesh and Menoth White Base.

2
Shade the lines and recesses of the face by adding Sanguine Highlight and a dot of Mixing Medium to the base color and applying thin coats of shadow.

3
Mix Battledress Green with some more of the base color and some Mixing Medium. Apply another thin shade using this color.

4
Refine the expression by applying thin lines of Sanguine Highlight mixed with Battledress Green to key parts of the face.

5
Highlight by adding Menoth White Highlight to the base mixture and applying it to the raised areas of the face.

6
Finally, apply Menoth White Highlight to the tips of the ears, nose, and brow and to the top of bald heads.

WHITE ARMOR

The white plates of Iosan armor can seem a bit tricky to paint at first, but with a little practice you'll have them looking great in no time. It is helpful to apply your paint in multiple thin coats rather than one or two heavy coats. Also make sure to separate each plate with a line of deep shadow to achieve the best results.

1 Basecoat the armor in Morrow White mixed with a couple of drops of Underbelly Blue.

2 Add Cryx Bane Highlight and a drop of Mixing Medium to the base color and apply it as shading.

3 Mix small amounts of Greatcoat Grey, Exile Blue, and Thamar Black to the previous color and apply it as the final shading.

4 Thin Morrow White with Mixing Medium and water and apply it to the armor plates as a highlight.

AQUA GLOW

There is a subtle aqua glow around the power nodes and vents of the Iosan weapons and armor. To achieve this effect use a mixture of equal parts Necrotite Green, Arcane Blue, and Carnal Pink. Water down the mixture and carefully apply it to the glowing recesses. With some practice you should be able to take advantage of the thinness of the paint by allowing it to flow easily into the channels sculpted into the figure.

KHAKI DRAB

Many of the Iosan models feature a tertiary khaki drab color. It is most commonly seen on the belts crisscrossing the midsection of many models.

1 Basecoat the area using Battledress Green. A few thin coats should produce solid coverage.

2 For your first layer of shadows, mix Sanguine Base with the base color. The continued use of Sanguine Base unifies the color palette.

3 Mix equal parts Sanguine Base and Umbral Umber for the final shading.

4 Begin highlighting with a mix of Battledress Green and Rucksack Tan.

5 Add Underbelly Blue to the mixture from the previous step and apply it as a final highlight.

OLIVE DRAB

We painted many of the pouches on the Iosan infantry in an olive color to set them apart from the other elements of the model without drawing attention away from the important areas.

1 Basecoat the pouch with an equal mixture of Ordic Olive and Cryx Bane Base.

2 Mix equal parts Cryx Bane Base and Battlefield Brown for the first layer of shading.

3 Mix Battlefield Brown with Coal Black and apply it in a series of lines to shade and define the pouch.

4 Return to your base color and add Rucksack Tan to the mixture. Use this color to highlight the pouches.

5 Mix Frostbite with the previous highlight mixture and apply it as the final highlight.

MILITARY GREEN

The majority of the clothing worn by the Iosan military is a muted military green. We wanted to add some warmth to the shadows of this green to add some character to the otherwise neutral Iosan color palette.

1

The basecoat color for this military green is an equal mixture of Traitor Green and Trollblood Base. A couple of thin layers should give you solid coverage.

2

Add Cryx Bane Base to the base color for the first layer of shading.

3

For the next shade layer add Sanguine Base to the paint mixture from the previous step. Aim for a color that is slightly more red than green.

4

The first highlight stage uses a mixture of the base color and Midlund Flesh. The warmth of the flesh tone contributes to an interesting and unique green.

5

For the final highlights, add Underbelly Blue to the mixture from the previous step. Apply this mixture to the raised folds and trim of the clothing.

SHINY TURQUOISE METAL

Adding a little bit of color to the Iosan metallic paint serves to tie the metal areas in with the overall palette of the model. Use ink to color the metallics so the shine of the metal is not reduced.

1 For the basecoat use three drops of Radiant Platinum mixed with one drop of Blue Ink, one drop of Turquoise Ink, and three drops of Armor Wash.

2 Use a mixture of Blue Ink, Turquoise Ink, and Armor Wash for the shading.

3 Apply highlights by reclaiming areas covered by the shading with Radiant Platinum.

4 To smooth the transition of color, mix a glaze of three parts Turquoise Ink, one part Blue Ink, one part Armor Wash, and eight parts water and apply it to the surface.

5 Apply Quick Silver to the edges of the blade to give the impression of light glinting off polished metal.

DARK PURPLE METAL

We painted the power nodes and sword hilts a darker metallic purple. The purple and green complement each other well without distracting from the overall composition.

1 Start with a basecoat mixture of three drops of Pig Iron, two drops of Red Ink, and one drop of Blue Ink.

2 Shade the metal with a mix of two drops of Blue Ink, one drop of Red Ink, three drops of Armor Wash, and a small amount of Thamar Black.

3 Apply Cold Steel as a highlight to the edges and raised areas.

GREY LEATHER

The arms, legs, and neck portions of many of the Iosan models are covered with interlocking bands of leather. We painted these bands in a cool grey that has relatively the same value as the military green so it does not compete for attention. Note the first stage of shading and highlights accentuates the roundness of the shape, and the second separates the bands from one another.

1 Start with a basecoat of Greatcoat Grey.

2 Add Sanguine Base and Umbral Umber to the basecoat and apply some thin shadow layers.

3 Use a mixture of Sanguine Base, Umbral Umber, and Coal Black for the crevices between bands and deep shadows.

4 Use Greatcoat Grey mixed with Cryx Bane Highlight for the first highlight stage.

5 Add Frostbite to the previous mix and use the resulting color to define the final highlights.

PLATINUM BLONDE HAIR

Many of the elves among the ranks of the Retribution sport unusual hair colors that you may not have encountered before as a painter. Platinum blonde is one of the more common hair colors among Iosans and is a perfect place to start.

1

Apply a solid basecoat of Menoth White Base mixed with Trollblood Highlight to achieve a yellowish grey.

2

Add some Turquoise Ink to the basecoat mixture and apply it as a shade to the hair.

3

Apply a second shade of Bastion Grey to separate the strands of hair and add depth.

4

Lastly, apply highlights to the ridges of the hair using a mixture of the basecoat color and Menoth White Highlight.

BROWN-PURPLE FADE

Adding subtle unnatural color to normal hair tones is a great way to add character and mystery to your elves. This fade from warm brown to deep purple is at once unusual and elegant.

1

Apply a simple basecoat of Gun Corps Brown.

2

Apply a mixture of Beaten Purple and Bootstrap Leather to the recesses of the hair for the first shade.

3

Use a mixture of Beaten Purple and Coal Black as the second shade on the tips of the hair.

4

Lastly mix together equal parts Gun Corps Brown, Rucksack Tan, and Ember Orange. Use the resulting color to highlight the roots of the hair.

ELECTRIC BLUE HAIR

Kaelyssa's hair is a vibrant electric blue. We hope you'll allow yourself to be inspired to create your own unique hair colors and fades.

1 Mix Menoth White Base with Sulfuric Yellow and apply a solid basecoat to the entire head of hair.

2 Next apply Turquoise Ink to the recesses of the hair so the strands visually separate from one another.

3 Deepen the shadows and accent the shape of the hairstyle by adding a second shade with Blue Ink.

4 Darken the hair tips with a glaze mixture of Thamar Black, Turquoise Ink, Blue Ink, Mixing Medium, and water.

GREY-MAGENTA FADE

With this unique hair color we create a fade from a neutral grey to bold magenta. It is a striking look that will immediately draw the eye.

1 The basecoat for this color fade is a mixture of Trollblood Highlight and Carnal Pink.

2 Shade the recesses of the hair with a mixture of equal parts Beast Hide, Murderous Magenta, and Bastion Grey.

3 Shade the tips of the hair using a mixture of Greatcoat Grey and Murderous Magenta.

4 Apply highlights using a mixture of equal parts Trollblood Highlight, Menoth White Highlight, and Moldy Ochre.

RETRIBUTION
GALLERY

DAWNLORD VYROS
Warcaster

KAELYSSA, NIGHT'S WHISPER
Warcaster

ADEPTIS RAHN
Warcaster

RAVYN, ETERNAL LIGHT
Warcaster

GARRYTH, BLADE OF RETRIBUTION
Warcaster

CHIMERA
Light Myrmidon

NAYL
Solo

ARCANIST
Solo

HYDRA
Heavy Myrmidon

DAWNGUARD INVICTORS
Unit

SOULLESS ESCORT
Unit Attachment

MANTICORE
Heavy Myrmidon

DAWNGUARD SENTINELS
Unit

GRIFFON
Light Myrmidon

MAGE HUNTER COMMANDER
Unit Attachment

MAGE HUNTER STRIKE FORCE
Unit

GORGON
Light Myrmidon

MAGE HUNTER ASSASSIN
Solo

**EIRYSS,
MAGE HUNTER OF IOS**
Solo

**EIRYSS,
ANGEL OF RETRIBUTION**
Epic Solo

PHOENIX
Heavy Myrmidon

HOUSE SHYEEL BATTLE MAGES
Unit

NARN,
MAGE HUNTER OF IOS
Solo

GHOST SNIPER
Solo

HOUSE SHYEEL
MAGISTER
Solo